FEAR NO EVIL

Warren McWilliams

Learning Activities and Leader Guide
by Diane K. Noble

LifeWay Press®
Nashville, Tennessee

ISBN 1-4158-2803-2

This book is the resource for course CG-1104 in the category Baptist Doctrine
in the Christian Growth Study Plan.

Dewey Decimal classification: 233
Subject headings: GOOD AND EVIL \ PROVIDENCE AND GOVERNMENT OF GOD \
CHRISTIAN LIFE

Cover design: Ed Crawford

Unless otherwise noted, all Scripture quotations are taken from
the Holman Christian Standard Bible®, copyright © 1999, 2000, 2001, 2002, 2003
by Holman Bible Publishers. Used by permission.

Scripture quotations identified NIV are from the Holy Bible, New International Version,
copyright © 1973, 1978, 1984 by International Bible Society. Used by permission.

Scripture quotations marked NEB are taken from The New English Bible.
Copyright © Oxford University Press and Cambridge University Press, 1961, 1970.
All rights reserved. Reprinted by permission.

Scripture quotations marked GNT are from the Good News Translation in Today's English
Version—Second Edition Copyright © 1992 by American Bible Society. Used by permission.

Scripture quotations marked KJV are from the King James Version of the Bible.

We believe that the Bible has God for its author; salvation for its end; and truth, without any mixture of error,
for its matter and that all Scripture is totally true and trustworthy. The 2000 statement
of The Baptist Faith and Message is our doctrinal guideline.

To order additional copies of this resource: write to
LifeWay Church Resources Customer Service; One LifeWay Plaza; Nashville, TN 37234-0113;
fax (615) 251-5933; phone toll free (800) 458-2772; order online at www.lifeway.com;
or visit the LifeWay Christian Store serving you.

Printed in the United States of America

Leadership and Adult Publishing
LifeWay Church Resources
One LifeWay Plaza
Nashville, TN 37234-0175

Contents

The Author

WARREN McWILLIAMS occupies the Auguie Henry Chair of Bible in the Joe L. Ingram School of Christian Service at Oklahoma Baptist University, where he has taught Bible, theology, and ethics since 1976. A graduate of Oklahoma Baptist University, Southern Baptist Theological Seminary, and Vanderbilt University, McWilliams has served on church staffs in Oklahoma and Tennessee. He regularly teaches and preaches in area churches. He and his wife, Patty, have two adult daughters, Amy and Karen.

McWilliams is a frequent contributor to Sunday School curriculum for LifeWay Christian Resources of the Southern Baptist Convention, and he has written articles for *Holman Bible Dictionary* and *Mercer Dictionary of the Bible*. He has published academic articles and book reviews in several journals. His previous books include *Free in Christ: The New Testament Understanding of Freedom*, *The Passion of God: Divine Suffering in Contemporary Protestant Theology*, *When You Walk Through the Fire*, *Christ and Narcissus: Prayer in a Self-Centered World*, and *Dear Chris: Letters on the Life of Faith*. His latest release is *Where Is the God of Justice? Biblical Perspectives on Suffering*.

McWilliams has been intrigued by the topic of evil and suffering throughout his ministry. He frequently preaches and teaches about the topic, knowing that many Christians wrestle with the relationship between their faith in God and the struggles of life.

DIANE K. NOBLE wrote the learning activities and the leader guide for this study. Noble is the director of discipleship and women's ministries at First Baptist Church in Harrisonville, Missouri. Noble has an extensive background in curriculum development and has facilitated numerous conferences and professional workshops. She holds undergraduate and graduate degrees in education and administration.

Introduction

Dates are often more than mere numbers on a calendar page. For example, May 31, 1968, is one of my favorite dates because it is the day I married Patty. Other dates, however, remind me of tragic events. Along with millions of other Americans, I will always remember September 11, 2001, because of the terrorist attacks that killed thousands. December 26, 2004, is the date of the massive earthquake that produced the tsunamis that killed almost 300,000 in southern Asia. As you read this book, you will likely think of dates that remind you of clashes with evil or experiences with suffering.

The topics of evil, suffering, and God's providence should concern all Christians. There are at least four reasons believers need to explore these complex topics.

We all suffer and wonder why painful experiences happen to us. Perhaps you have experienced grief over the death of a friend or a relative. You may have a physical or spiritual problem that causes you continual agony. In our world the possibilities of pain are almost endless. I hope this study will help you understand your pain.

The Bible is relevant to our experiences with evil and suffering. The Bible is the supreme authority for our beliefs and behavior. Evil and suffering are central issues throughout the Bible. Because people of faith have often been perplexed about their troubles, many biblical writers address the concerns of this book. This study is essentially an exploration of the biblical views of evil and suffering.

Biblical teachings on evil and suffering are best understood in context. Many books mention the Bible's understanding of suffering, but very few give a systematic study of the biblical views. Some books have tried to address this need, but they are either oriented primarily to a scholarly audience or are not as comprehensive as this book. I have written primarily for laypersons who want to know what the Bible says about evil and suffering. By analyzing large blocks of material, such as the Gospels or Paul's letters, I have attempted to examine key biblical themes and texts within their historical contexts. Although we will trace some basic themes throughout our study, examining these topics in their biblical contexts will deepen our understanding of the Bible's message on evil and suffering.

This book emphasizes God's relationship to evil and suffering. Many people immediately think of God when they begin to suffer. Sometimes we are angry with God. Sometimes we plead with God for help. Three questions about God will be central to our study:
- Why does God allow or cause suffering?
- How does God help us when we suffer?
- What does God expect us to do about the suffering of others?

The study will not address the entire biblical doctrine of God, but it will highlight His characteristics that relate to the problems of evil and suffering. My main thesis is that God identifies with human suffering and strengthens us in our suffering. Because a Christian's character should mirror God's character, we should reach out with compassion and comfort to those around us who are suffering.

This short study cannot answer all of our questions about human pain and divine providence, but a distinctively Christian view of God will help us respond creatively and appropriately to suffering—our suffering and that of other people. In Psalm 23 David's confidence was based on his faith in God:

> *Even though I walk*
> *through the valley of the shadow of death,*
> *I will fear no evil,*
> *for you are with me.* Psalm 23:4, NIV

The night before He was crucified, Jesus comforted His disciples: "'You will have suffering in this world. Be courageous! I have conquered the world'" (John 16:33). The God who was supremely revealed in Jesus is the God we worship and serve; He will walk with us through all of the dark valleys of life.

Chapter 1

The Fiery Ordeal

A S I READ THE MORNING NEWSPAPER several years ago, one letter in the "Dear Abby" column caught my eye. The letter dealt with several issues we will encounter in our study of the biblical views of evil and suffering.

Dear Abby:

My 14-year-old son was killed in a tragic accident seven months ago, and I am just now beginning to come out of my numbness and shock. Throughout the ordeal, friends, family, and acquaintances tried to comfort me. Some succeeded, while others failed miserably.

The following comments are words that did not help at all. I realize that everyone was trying to be kind, but there are certain words bereaved parents do not want to hear:

1. "I know just how you feel. I lost my mother, father, husband, brother, sister, and so forth." These words are so hollow to a parent who has lost a child. Unless they have suffered the loss of a child, there is no way on earth they can know how you feel.

2. "It was God's will." I am no more (or less) religious than the average person, but if it was "God's will" to take my son at 14 and end his young life, then I want no part of a God who could be so cruel.

3. "God needed him more than you did." How inadequate that made me feel, as though something was lacking within myself. If I had needed him more, would he still be alive?

4. "These things happen for a reason." What reason? There is no reason good enough to explain why I had to suffer the loss of my child.

5. "You can have another child" or "At least you have your other children." This is really cold and cruel. Children are individuals, and no child can replace the child who has died.

Now for some words that comforted me: a simple and heartfelt, "I'm so sorry." Many people hugged me, held my hand, or cried with me. No words were spoken, but they were there for me when I needed them.—Linda Lancaster

Linda's comments intrigued me because they were like many I hear every day. As a professor in a university department of religion, I often talk with students who are perplexed by the hurt and loss in the world. When I served on church staffs, I heard similar concerns from the church and community. Probably everyone—Christian or non-Christian—has voiced or felt anxiety over evil and suffering.

This book will present a systematic study of the biblical views of evil and suffering. In this chapter we will lay the groundwork for our study by addressing these basic questions: What are evil and suffering? How do we understand the Bible's teachings on evil and suffering? What is God's relationship to human suffering?

What Are Evil and Suffering?

Evil
People, powers, influences, and actions that oppose God and His purposes

Evil and suffering are not the same thing, though they clearly relate to each other. *Evil* may be defined as *people, powers, influences, and actions that oppose God and His purposes*. In other words, evil is anything that displeases God. The term encompasses all kinds of events and actions. The destruction of millions of Jews during World War II was evil, but so is any sin I commit today.

Suffering is the deeply personal response to a catastrophic or devastating event that brings overwhelming turmoil to our physical, emotional, or spiritual well-being. Evil actions may produce suffering, but suffering may also result from physical illness, mental anguish, spiritual turmoil, war, grief, unrequited love, accidents, abuse, hurricanes, tornadoes, and many other painful experiences.[1]

Suffering
The deeply personal response to a catastrophic or devastating event that brings overwhelming turmoil to our physical, emotional, or spiritual well-being

1. Check the words that you associate with suffering.

☐ **Agony**   ☐ **Distress**   ☐ **Anguish**
☐ **Hardship**   ☐ **Dissatisfaction**   ☐ **Displeasure**
☐ **Misfortune**   ☐ **Pain**   ☐ **Abuse**
☐ **Irritation**   ☐ **Anger**   ☐ **Disappointment**

Circle word(s) that relate to suffering you have experienced.

Let's begin by looking at two traditional types of suffering that will help us classify the scriptural examples of suffering we will observe throughout our study.

Moral suffering. Moral suffering is caused by human sin. This type of suffering comes (1) from suffering the consequences of our own actions or (2) from being an innocent victim of someone else's sin.

Several years ago, for example, a friend was driving back to our town when a drunk driver crossed the center line of the highway and slammed into his car. My friend was severely injured, and the drunk driver sustained injuries as well. Both endured the consequences of the intoxicated driver's sin. Both suffered physical pain and suffering. My friend lost considerable time from his career while he recuperated, and the drunk driver faced legal and criminal penalties for her sin.

2. Check examples of moral suffering.
☐ **a. A random shooting takes the lives of innocent victims.**
☐ **b. A hurricane hits the coast, causing injuries.**
☐ **c. A child is kidnapped and is physically or psychologically damaged.**
☐ **d. A person files for bankruptcy after losing most personal assets through gambling debt.**
☐ **e. A person gets leukemia and dies.**

Doctrine of Retribution
The view that actions have consequences

Choices *a*, *c*, and *d* are examples of moral suffering. The Bible presents numerous examples of moral suffering that results from our own actions. In fact, throughout our study we will see that a major biblical interpretation of moral suffering is the doctrine of retribution—the view that our actions have consequences. Paul reinforced the doctrine of retribution when he wrote, "Whatever a man sows he will also reap" (Gal. 6:7).

"A little sleep, a little slumber,
a little folding of the arms to rest,
and your poverty will come like a robber,
your need, like a bandit."
Proverbs 6:10-11

3. In the proverbs in the margin, underline words that describe the consequences of laziness.

"The diligent hand will rule,
but laziness will lead to forced labor."
Proverbs 12:24

The Bible also notes examples of moral suffering that results when innocent victims are harmed by someone else's sin. An individual's poverty, for example, might be the result of someone else's greed rather than the person's laziness. A diligent, responsible worker might not prosper because his employer is corrupt. The prophet Amos criticized the wealthy Hebrews of the eighth century B.C. for oppressing the poor, thereby causing them to suffer:

"The slacker craves,
yet has nothing,
but the diligent is fully satisfied."
Proverbs 13:4

> *They sell a righteous person for silver*
> *and a needy person for a pair of sandals.*
> *They trample the heads of the poor*
> *on the dust of the ground*
> *and block the path of the needy.*
> Amos 2:6-7

Most suffering probably comes directly and primarily from human behavior. C. S. Lewis once said that four-fifths of our suffering is caused by our sin.[2] Scripture supports this view.

"Laziness induces deep sleep,
and a lazy person will go hungry."
Proverbs 19:15

4. Read the following passages in your Bible. Match each reference with the form of suffering it describes.

____ 1. Psalm 106:43   **a. Life will fall apart, collapse.**
____ 2. Proverbs 29:6   **b. Beaten down by sin**
____ 3. Isaiah 30:13   **c. Death**
____ 4. Jeremiah 17:3-4   **d. Caught by sin**
____ 5. Romans 6:23   **e. Loss of God's inheritance and blessing**

These Scriptures illustrate the fact that the primary cause of moral suffering is sin—using our freedom of choice to rebel against God. Wars, murder, theft, drunkenness, and other forms of human rebellion result from using freedom for evil rather than good. You should have matched the references this way: 1. *b*, 2. *d*, 3. *a*, 4. *e*, 5. *c*.

Sin
Using our freedom of choice to rebel against God

5. To what extent do you think God is responsible for moral suffering? Mark an *X* on the continuum.

DIRECTLY RESPONSIBLE   **INDIRECTLY RESPONSIBLE**   **NOT RESPONSIBLE**

We can't blame God for our failure to exercise our freedom responsibly. Ultimately, God may be responsible for suffering because He created a world in which humans have limited yet genuine freedom, but God is not directly accountable for our moral failures. We are. In our example of the drunk driver, the driver was free to get drunk and cause suffering. She made a choice. If I were her parent, I might be indirectly responsible for her behavior. After all, some would argue that I allowed her to use the car. I never intended, however, for her to get drunk or drive recklessly. So is it fair to assume that God is responsible for Hitler's atrocities? For war? For the devastation caused when a father leaves his wife and children?

Natural suffering. Natural suffering is caused by the forces of nature. The tsunami that struck south Asia on December 26, 2004, provides a tragic example. Almost 300,000 people died as a result of tidal waves that hit Sri Lanka, Indonesia, and other countries.[3] Each year thousands more die because of disease, earthquakes, tornadoes, hurricanes, floods, lightning, and mudslides—all catalysts of natural suffering.

Many find natural suffering even more difficult to understand than moral suffering. Although we have a hard time comprehending why Hitler was so evil, we know that people can hate so deeply that they want to hurt others. But we may not understand why God allows tornadoes to ravage Oklahoma each spring or a tsunami to kill thousands. Seldom are we inclined to see the forces of nature as causes of our suffering, because we assume that the wind, sea, and other natural forces are not conscious, free beings.

6. Which description matches your understanding of the cause of natural disasters?

☐ **Natural disasters result from random occurrences in the physical laws of nature that occur apart from God's control.**

☐ **While God is in complete control of nature, we live in a fallen world that includes natural disasters and disease.**

☐ **Though I may not understand His purpose, God is in command of the universe and has a direct hand in any and all natural disasters.**

Natural disasters puzzle many believers. When I was a senior in college, I conducted a psychological study of children with terminal diseases such as leukemia. Although I tried to carry out an objective, scientific study, I was perplexed by the fundamental question of why these innocent children had a disease at all. Why did they have to suffer?

The Bible mentions relatively few cases of natural suffering, compared to moral suffering. Perhaps this relative silence adds to our frustration. We tend to think that if our pain is not caused by our sin or someone else's, then God must be causing it.

> We tend to think that if our pain is not caused by our sin or someone else's, then God must be causing it.

As we continue our study together, we will see that the Bible includes examples of both moral and natural suffering. We will witness human reactions to each type, gain clues about their causes, and learn how God relates to those who experience these ordeals.

How Do We Understand the Bible's Teachings on Evil and Suffering?

We can't properly evaluate biblical teachings on evil and suffering without trying to interpret these teachings within their historical contexts. Therefore, I have organized this study in terms of the broad sweep of biblical history, beginning with Genesis and ending with Revelation.

I learned long ago that a biblical text without a context is a proof text. A proof text is a statement that seems to prove an idea but actually says something quite different when considered in its proper context. I like the example I used in another book: "Lincoln reportedly said, 'You can fool all the people some of the time.' By itself, this statement leaves the impression that Lincoln was very cynical about human nature. In fact, when you look at this quotation in the context of Lincoln's larger thought, it means just the opposite. Lincoln actually said, 'You can fool all the people some of the time, and some of the people all of the time, but you cannot fool all the people all of the time.' Lincoln actually had a high regard for our ability to discern the true from the false."[4]

As we interpret the biblical views of evil and suffering, we need to remind ourselves of two contexts.

The context of history and culture. Considering the historical-cultural context of the author and of the original audience will help us discover what the passage meant to the first readers. Only by discovering the original meaning can we learn what the passage says to our generation. We can increase our understanding of the biblical teachings on evil and suffering if we consider each book's teaching in its historical context. Let's look at an example.

> We can increase our understanding of the biblical teachings on evil and suffering if we consider each book's teaching in its historical context.

7. Read in your Bible the account of Elkanah and Hannah in 1 Samuel 1:1-18. Then answer the questions.

What type of marriage arrangement was commonly practiced in Elkanah's day (v. 2)? _____

What was Hannah's plight (v. 5)? _____

_____

What added to Hannah's suffering (vv. 6-7)? _____

_____

What words are used to describe Hannah's suffering (vv. 8-11)?

_____

How did the historical context of Hannah's situation make her anguish more intense than it might be in today's culture?

_____

Understanding the historical context of this passage helps us grasp the extreme suffering Hannah experienced. The Old Testament practice of polygamy was never God's intention for marriage. Those who practiced it often encountered anguish and suffering that they may not have attributed directly to their cultural practice. Hannah's barrenness caused her humiliation, and Peninnah only added to Hannah's grief.

The context of the author's message. We must also consider each author's teaching in the context of his larger message. The quotation by Lincoln was misleading until we saw the larger context. Likewise, we can misunderstand biblical quotations on evil and suffering if we do not recognize the author's major emphasis. For example, a biblical author may stress God's power to remind readers that God can help us in times of distress. Taken out of context, the emphasis on God's power might lead us to expect Him to alter every situation to suit our personal preferences. However, the context gives us clues about how to interpret the teaching:

> **We must consider each author's teaching in the context of his larger message.**

- If our suffering is the consequence of our sin, the author's broader message will show that we should not expect God to remove that suffering. For example, Abraham apparently realized that God must destroy Sodom because of its wickedness (see Gen. 18:22-33).
- If our suffering is caused by someone else's sin, the larger context will encourage us that the situation can be altered. For example, the Hebrew prophets often consoled the oppressed and blamed their suffering on the rich and powerful.
- If the author's general purpose is to convict us of our sins, he tells us to accept the consequences of our actions.
- If the author's purpose is to console us in our innocent suffering, he tells us to expect God and others to intervene to help.

Examining the context of each Bible passage will reveal what the biblical writers intended to teach us about our experiences with evil and suffering.

What Is God's Relationship to Human Suffering?

The Bible frequently uses the image of fire to depict suffering. Fire is an appropriate image. If you put your hand into fire, it will hurt! A familiar biblical account of a fiery ordeal is found in Daniel 3.

Nebuchadnezzar was about to have Daniel's three friends thrown into a fiery furnace because they would not worship a golden image. The conversation between the king and the three men raises key themes about the way God relates to human suffering.

8. Read Daniel 3:13-18 in your Bible and check one answer to each question.

What was so arrogant about King Nebuchadnezzar's question to Shadrach, Meshach, and Abednego?
☐ He assumed that their God was not as powerful as his gods.
☐ He assumed that no god was powerful enough to save them from the fire.
☐ He assumed that their God was only one god among many.

What did the response of the three friends demonstrate about their belief about God?
☐ God might not exist, but if He did, He could act on their behalf.
☐ God would rescue them from the pain of the fiery furnace.
☐ God was powerful enough to deliver them, whether or not He did.

Based on this passage, what do you believe about God's power in times of suffering?
☐ If God doesn't rescue me from suffering, He is not powerful.
☐ God is powerful enough to save me, and I trust that He will.
☐ God is powerful, and I can trust Him when I suffer.

When We Suffer, God Is All-Powerful

When Nebuchadnezzar learned that Shadrach, Meshach, and Abednego refused to worship the idol, he declared that they would be thrown into the furnace and arrogantly asked, "'Who is the god who can rescue you from my power?'" (Dan. 3:15). The key issue in this conversation was power. Nebuchadnezzar assumed that these Hebrews worshiped a weak God. Indeed, the historical situation seems to support his assumption. Some scholars argue that people in those times were more concerned about the relative power of many gods than the existence or nonexistence of a single deity. Because the Babylonians had defeated the Hebrews and had taken

"'Who is the god who can rescue you from my power?'"
Daniel 3:15

some of them into captivity, the Babylonians naturally assumed that their gods were stronger. But the three Hebrews firmly believed that their God—the only true God—had the power necessary to deliver them: "'If we are thrown into the blazing furnace, the God we serve is able to save us from it'" (Dan. 3:17, NIV). In this bold statement Daniel's friends affirmed that God is powerful.

The Bible often affirms this characteristic of God. For example, when Sarah laughed at the announcement of her pregnancy, God asked, "'Is anything impossible for the LORD?'" (Gen. 18:14). When the Hebrews worried that God had deserted them or that He was impotent, God responded,

"Was my arm too short to ransom you?
Do I lack the strength to rescue you?" Isaiah 50:2, NIV

After announcing Jesus' conception to the virgin Mary, Gabriel reminded her, "'Nothing will be impossible with God'"(Luke 1:37). After the three men survived the fiery furnace, even Nebuchadnezzar acknowledged the power of their Deliverer (see Dan. 3:29).

Christians generally believe that God is all-powerful, or omnipotent. The Bible clearly teaches that God's power is unrivaled. God's use of power is always good because His nature is loving and good. His power always operates from His loving nature.

> "'There is no other god who is able to deliver like this.'"
> Daniel 3:29

Omnipotence
God's unlimited power to do what is within His holy and righteous character

9. Read the following verses in your Bible. Check the one that most closely describes your understanding of God's power.
☐ **Psalm 89:13-14**
☐ **Psalm 90:11-12**
☐ **Isaiah 40:10-11**

Explain your choice. _____

_____

Throughout our study you will probably find yourself asking, *If God is omnipotent, isn't He responsible for everything that happens, including all suffering?* We can begin answering that question by examining two common misconceptions of God's responsibility for human suffering. Both are based on distortions of the biblical understanding of God's power. Although a few proof texts might support these extreme views, we will find that a proper reading of these passages in context will not support either view.

Misconception 1: God is totally responsible for suffering. Some Christians emphasize God's sovereignty over the world by using biblical texts to suggest that everything—good and bad—happens as a direct result of His power.

Sovereignty
God's unlimited rule over His creation

10. Read the verses in the margin. What do these verses seem to suggest?
☐ **All suffering can be attributed to God.**
☐ **God is not responsible for suffering.**

" 'Who made the human mouth? Who makes him mute or deaf, seeing or blind? Is it not I, the LORD*?' "*
Exodus 4:11

Passages such as these, taken out of context, suggest that God directly causes physical handicaps and all disasters. This viewpoint led someone to tell the woman who wrote "Dear Abby" that her son's death was God's will.

The view that God directly wills and causes each case of suffering is a dangerous interpretation of Scripture. In general, the Bible teaches that God is ultimately in control in the course of events. When you read biblical texts that seem to attribute all difficulty to God, keep in mind that in both the Old and New Testaments, people of faith lived in polytheistic cultures. Because their culture adopted many gods, these people had no trouble believing in deity. For them the real issue was not the existence of gods but the relative strength of their gods. When God said He brings disaster or makes people blind, He was primarily stressing His role as the only true God—the only Deity with the power to create and act. When we ask, "Why is this happening?" we normally look for a physical or psychological cause. People in biblical times looked to a deity as the cause—God or Baal, God or Marduk, God or Aton, and so on. God consistently told the covenant people, "I am in ultimate control."

"I form light and create darkness, I make success and create disaster; I, the LORD*, do all these things."*
Isaiah 45:7

"If a disaster occurs in a city, hasn't the LORD *done it?"*
Amos 3:6

Although God ultimately controls whatever happens to us, the Bible also teaches that people have free will. God gives humans freedom and allows us to influence our lives by our choices. The Hebrew religious leaders, for example, repeatedly communicated the Hebrews' options and the consequences of those choices. The key here is that the choices are real. God was not playing games with the Hebrews. God had set the boundaries for their choices, but the direct cause of much of their suffering was their decision to sin. Our God has a perfect will and a permissive will. His perfect will may be for someone to be a hospital administrator on an international mission field. If the person refuses to take the actions that will lead her to that vocation, God will allow her the freedom to rebel against His perfect plan. He permits some things to happen because He created us as free beings, and He will not arbitrarily infringe on the freedom He has given us.

11. Study in your Bible the following passages about choices to live outside God's perfect will. Record your findings.

Passage	God's Will	Choice Made	Consequence
Genesis 2:15-17	_____ _____	_____ _____	_____ _____
Genesis 3:6,23-24	_____ _____	_____ _____	_____ _____
Matthew 19:16-26	_____ _____	_____ _____	_____ _____

> When we choose our will over His, suffering is inevitable.

God is just. Although He allows us to choose whether to obey Him, He will not allow us to escape the consequences of our decisions. When we choose our will over His, suffering is inevitable. Our rebellious choices and the suffering caused by those choices grieve God. Like a loving parent, He will discipline us to regain our obedience.

12. Mark each statement *T* for true or *F* for false. Check your answers by reviewing what you have read.
____ God directly causes all suffering.
____ God is ultimately in control of events.
____ People have free will.
____ Free will prevents us from suffering.
____ God sometimes infringes on our free will.
____ We suffer when we choose our will over God's.

Misconception 2: God is not at all responsible for suffering. In the ancient world this outlook, called dualism, represented an alternative to the Christian faith. Dualism is the view that all reality is composed of two types of substance—spiritual and material, good and evil, light and dark. Dualists see suffering as caused not by God but by an evil force or power. They believe two equally powerful beings are engaged in a struggle for control of the world.

The Old Testament offers God's omnipotence as a clear safeguard against dualism. Although the Hebrews were aware of the power of the Devil, they never highlighted his role as the cause of human suffering. The early Christians also refused to attribute humanity's suffering primarily to Satan. They rejected the temptation to say that God does the good and Satan does the evil.

Dualism may seem like an odd view to people today. Our natural reaction to suffering is to blame God or at least appeal to Him for help. However, Christians who become preoccupied with the subject of Satan and demons may exhibit a dangerous tendency toward dualism. It is possible to exalt Satan's role in causing our problems to the extent that we implicitly reject God's omnipotence. The Bible clearly indicates that God alone is omnipotent. Satan is a created being who misused his freedom similarly to the way Adam did. Although Satan may have enough power to cause problems, the ultimate responsibility for the world belongs to God.

13. Read what Jesus said about His power and authority in the following two passages. Then fill in the blanks.

Read Luke 10:17-20. Jesus watched Satan _____ from heaven. Jesus gives His disciples authority over ____ the enemy's power.

Read Matthew 16:18-19. The forces of Hades (hell) will not _____ the church (believers).

Read 1 Peter 5:8-11 in the margin. Circle strategies for responding to Satan's attacks. Underline four things God will do for us.

In the New Testament the dualist threat took the form of Gnosticism. This belief system limited God's power and responsibility

Dualism
The belief that good and evil are equally powerful forces that operate in the universe

"Be sober! Be on the alert! Your adversary the Devil is prowling around like a roaring lion, looking for anyone he can devour. Resist him, firm in the faith, knowing that the same sufferings are being experienced by your brothers in the world. Now the God of all grace … will personally restore, establish, strengthen, and support you after you have suffered a little. To Him be the dominion forever."
1 Peter 5:8-11

Gnosticism
A first-century belief system claiming that the physical world is evil and the cause of all suffering

to the realm of the spiritual, asserting that God could not be contaminated with the evil physical world. Gnostics believed that all suffering is caused by living in the physical dimension of ordinary life. Gnostics blamed humanity's problems on the idea that good spiritual souls are trapped in evil physical bodies. By learning the secret knowledge *(gnosis)* offered by the Gnostics, humans could be delivered from the multitude of pains and problems they face. In later Gnostic speculation God did not even get the credit (blame, in their view) for creating the physical world. The physical world is the product of an evil deity, not the good God. Therefore, our suffering is caused by our involvement in the evil physical world, not by God's omnipotent control of the world. In the Gnostic view, God is responsible for good, not evil.

Some believers talk as if being free from this world and their bodies would solve everything. That is a Gnostic dualist position. Christian convictions about the goodness of the created world (see Gen. 1), Jesus' incarnation (see John 1), and the resurrection (see 1 Cor. 15) deny a dualistic explanation of suffering.

14. Identify two problems with claiming that God has no responsibility for our suffering.

_____

_____

When we deny God's role in suffering altogether, we might take a dualist stance that (1) rejects His omnipotence and (2) denies the goodness of the physical world. Topics such as God's nature, Satan's role in suffering, and human freedom will resurface throughout our study as we seek a biblical understanding of God's omnipotence.

When We Suffer, God Cares

Not only were Daniel's friends confident that God *could* help them because of His omnipotence, but they also expected that He *would* help them: "'If we are thrown into the blazing furnace, the God we serve is able to save us from it, and he will rescue us from your hand, O king'" (Dan. 3:17, NIV). These men firmly believed that their God was willing and able to save them from their suffering.

This Hebrew confidence that God cares about His people and will help them in their suffering is one of the most prominent themes in the Bible. When the first-century Christians prepared to face their own fiery ordeal, Peter encouraged them, "Cast all anxiety on him because he cares for you" (1 Pet. 5:7, NIV). Many people consider God's care, rather than His power, as the crux of God's relationship to suffering. Indeed, the technical term for a study of evil and suffering, *theodicy*, relates to God's character more than His power. *Theodicy* comes from the Greek words for *God (theos)* and *justice (dike)*. Theodicy addresses the question, Is God just? For many who suffer, the real dilemma is how to reconcile God's power and goodness. How can God be both good (just) and God (powerful)? To respond to these concerns, we need to explore the relationship between God's power (omnipotence) and His goodness (omnibenevolence).

Let's begin our investigation by highlighting two attributes of God that relate to His goodness: compassion and comfort. *Compassion* refers to God's identification with our suffering, while *comfort* refers to His action to strengthen and encourage us in our suffering. Although love is a prominent component of God's nature, at least one biblical author, Paul, saw God's qualities of compassion and comfort as especially important in relation to human suffering: "Praise be to the God and Father of our Lord Jesus Christ, the Father of compassion and the God of all comfort, who comforts us in all our troubles" (2 Cor. 1:3-4, NIV).

Theodicy
An explanation of how evil exists in a world where God is all-good and all-powerful

Omnibenevolence
God's goodness

Compassion
God's identification with human suffering

Comfort
God's action to strengthen and encourage people who suffer

15. Fill in the blanks to complete the definitions.
Compassion is God's _____ with our suffering.
Comfort is God's _____ to strengthen us in suffering.

When Daniel's friends assured Nebuchadnezzar that their God would help them, they had faith that God knew of their plight and had compassion for them. Related to our term *sympathy, compassion* literally means *to suffer with*. The Bible consistently presents God as hearing and responding to His people's needs. The Exodus experience became the basic model for the Hebrews' view of God. When they were enslaved by the Egyptians, God cared: "God heard their groaning and he remembered his covenant with Abraham, with Isaac and with Jacob. So God looked on the Israelites and was concerned about them" (Ex. 2:24-25, NIV). When God gave the Hebrews the law, He reminded them, " 'I am compassionate' " (Ex. 22:27). God feels His people's pain as His own. The woman who wrote "Dear Abby" obviously believed that only someone with an identical experience could understand her feelings. The Bible affirms that God identifies with all who hurt. We are not alone when we suffer.

16. Think of a time when you were hurting. Describe how you experienced God's compassion—His identification with your suffering. _____

_____

Describe how you experienced God's comfort—His action to strengthen you. _____

_____

Some people feel that a good, compassionate God would not allow any suffering. A good God, they reason, would use His omnipotence to make sure we never suffer. However, the Bible doesn't teach that God promised to protect His people from all suffering.

"When the fiery ordeal arises among you to test you, don't be surprised by it, as if something unusual were happening to you. Instead, as you share in the sufferings of the Messiah rejoice, so that you may also rejoice with great joy at the revelation of His glory. If you are ridiculed for the name of Christ, you are blessed, because the Spirit of glory and of God rests on you."
1 Peter 4:12-14

17. Examine 1 Peter 4:12-14 in the margin. What should be our response to suffering for the cause of Christ?
☐ Try to escape   ☐ Rejoice   ☐ Fight back

Why should we respond this way?
☐ So that Christ will be glorified
☐ So that we will be happy

What is our standing before God when we suffer for Christ?
☐ Blessed   ☐ Exalted   ☐ Punished

Several New Testament passages suggest that the early Christians expected to suffer in the Roman Empire and that to avoid all suffering was a false hope. The Bible tells us what to do *when* we suffer, not *if* we suffer.

People who reject belief in God's compassion also point to innocent or undeserved suffering. As we have already seen, most people realize that because our actions have consequences, some suffering is deserved. But when the good guys lose and the bad guys win, many are deeply disturbed. Although the Bible does not speculate on this dilemma, it offers advice on how to respond practically to various types of injustice. And it never offers the option of choosing between a cruel, unjust God and no God at all.

Some people seem to assume that if injustice exists in the world, their only choice is to reject the idea of a loving God. As we saw in our discussion of omnipotence, God may be all-powerful yet willing to let humans exercise their freedom. At least moral suffering is possible with a God who is completely loving and compassionate. Those who reject God because He allows suffering may have a false view of God's power as well as His love. They seem to want a grandfatherly God who intends to keep us from all suffering yet who is dictatorial in His use of power. We could have such a just world if we were all robots, but the misuse of our human freedom always opens the door to suffering.

18. Check the true statement.
☐ **The existence of suffering means that God allows humans to exercise their freedom, which may result in suffering.**
☐ **The existence of suffering means that God is not compassionate.**

When We Suffer, God Helps

Shadrach, Meshach, and Abednego rightly believed that God could help them (omnipotence) and that He would help them (omnibenevolence). God would respond to their problem. He was willing and able to help. They also recognized that God's help might not come in the form of a miraculous intervention. They told Nebuchadnezzar, " 'Even if He does not rescue us, we want you as king to know that we will not serve your gods or worship the gold statue you set up' " (Dan. 3:18). As the incident unfolded, God protected them from injury, and Nebuchadnezzar saw a strange figure walking in the furnace with them (see Dan. 3:25).

God is capable of and committed to helping us in our suffering, and He has compassion when we suffer. Another aspect of God's response to suffering is comfort (see 2 Cor. 1:3-4). Our English

"Praise be to the God and Father of our Lord Jesus Christ, the Father of compassion and the God of all comfort, who comforts us in all our troubles."
2 Corinthians 1:3-4, NIV

word *comfort* has gained the connotation of consolation or cheering up. We have the impression that someone who comforts merely says soothing words to make us feel better. But the English word *comfort*, originally from Latin, meant *to make strong*. A true comforter is one who strengthens or encourages a sufferer.

If you grew up using the King James Version, you probably associate comfort with the Holy Spirit because of the way passages such as John 14:16 are translated. The Good News Translation in Today's English Version translates the Greek word as *Helper* instead of *Comforter* to recover some of the word's original meaning. The word *comfort* is often used in the Bible to describe God's role, whether as Father (see 2 Cor. 1:3-4), Son (see 1 John 2:1), or Holy Spirit.

Simply stating that God helps people in their suffering may leave us open to misunderstanding. We can illuminate the meaning of God's help or comfort by examining common misconceptions.

Some people misunderstand how God helps us. We have seen that many people expect God to eliminate all suffering. Since suffering exists, however, how does God act to remove it? We often forget that God did not remove the suffering of many people in the Bible. Paul, for example, suffered from a thorn in the flesh and asked for relief, but the thorn remained.

"A thorn in the flesh was given to me, a messenger of Satan to torment me so I would not exalt myself. Concerning this, I pleaded with the Lord three times to take it away from me. But He said to me, 'My grace is sufficient for you, for power is perfected in weakness.' Therefore, I will most gladly boast all the more about my weaknesses, so that Christ's power may reside in me. So because of Christ, I am pleased in weaknesses, in insults, in catastrophes, in persecutions, and in pressures. For when I am weak, then I am strong."
2 Corinthians 12:7-10

19. Read 2 Corinthians 12:7-10 in the margin and check your answers to the following.
Paul was given a thorn to keep him—
☐ **worried**   ☐ **humble**   ☐ **tormented**
What did God want to perfect in Paul?
☐ **Paul's power**   ☐ **Grace**   ☐ **Christ's power**
What did Paul finally do about the thorn in his flesh?
☐ **Gladly accepted it**   ☐ **Endured it**   ☐ **Removed it himself**

Paul wrote that the purpose of his thorn was to keep him humble. God did not remove the thorn so that Christ's power would be perfected in Paul's weakness. For this reason Paul gladly accepted his thorn and boasted in his weakness so that Christ's power would be evident in his life.

Scripture records other examples in which God did not remove the cause of suffering, but the example we find in Jesus is one of the most poignant. Jesus asked to escape the suffering He would endure: " 'Father, if You are willing, take this cup away from Me—nevertheless, not My will, but Yours, be done' " (Luke 22:42). But understanding that God's plan of redemption required His sacrifice, Jesus willingly accepted His inevitable suffering.

The Bible teaches that God always helps us, but His comfort may not come in the form we expect. We usually want a dramatic miracle to relieve suffering. God always sends help, but we do not always recognize it or appreciate it because we insist on a specific kind of aid. The account of Elijah has often reminded me that God does not always operate through the miraculous or the spectacular. At Mount Carmel Elijah saw God dramatically display His power by sending fire on Elijah's altar (see 1 Kings 18:38). Later on Mount Horeb God spoke to Elijah in "a soft whisper" (1 Kings 19:12) rather than in spectacular upheavals of nature such as the wind, the earthquake, or the fire. I suspect that God was trying to teach Elijah and us that He works through the ordinary as well as the extraordinary.

I once read about a man named Smith who was stranded on his roof during a flood. As the waters rose, a man in a canoe offered to rescue him, but Smith, confident that God would help him, refused to get in the canoe. Smith also refused help from a man in a motorboat and from a helicopter pilot. Later when Smith met God in heaven, he said: "I trusted You. Why didn't You help me?" God replied: "What did you expect? I sent a canoe, a motorboat, and a helicopter!" Although the story is meant to be humorous, it teaches a profound lesson: perhaps we accuse God of not helping us in our troubles because we do not recognize the help He sends.

20. Identify a time when you were able to see only in retrospect that God had been helping you.

_____

_____

Why were you initially unable to see His helping hand? _____

_____

> God always helps us, but His comfort may not come in the form we expect.

Which of the following actions would help you perceive God's intervention in the future? Check those you would use.
☐ **Viewing every circumstance as a way God may be intervening on your behalf**
☐ **Asking God to give you insight and discernment to see His hand**
☐ **Seeking the godly counsel of others to help you see where God may be acting**
☐ **Meditating on Scripture that relates to God's activity in your life**
☐ **Trusting that God will intervene on your behalf whether or not you perceive it**

Some people misunderstand whom God helps. Some people believe that God helps only a select few while allowing others to suffer. Several years ago my pastor and his teenage son both had medical problems. Because my pastor's problem involved his vocal cords, he was told he would need surgery unless he quit talking. Undaunted, he kept on talking, the church prayed for him, and the situation improved. The son, however, was diagnosed with curvature of the spine. The church also prayed for his recovery, but his situation did not improve. Surgery was necessary. Some people wondered, "Why did God help Jerry and not Joel?"

This misunderstanding of God's comfort overlaps with the first one because some people see only miraculous recovery as a sign of God's concern and help. Sometimes God helps by removing us from the suffering, but sometimes He helps by strengthening us in it. Unfortunately, some people have a very selfish view of God's comfort. Their attitude seems to be "God, if You help me, then I'll be loyal to You." Jacob's life illustrates this self-centered attitude. At one point he listed several conditions God must meet before Jacob would promise to follow Him (see Gen. 28:20-21). Daniel's three friends, on the other hand, were committed to God whether or not He miraculously intervened to rescue them.

Some people misunderstand when God will help. Many biblical authors express the sentiment of Psalm 119:82: "'When will You comfort me?'" Throughout the Bible we read that if justice does not prevail now, God will correct the situation in the future.

"Jacob made a vow: 'If God will be with me and watch over me on this journey, if He provides me with food to eat and clothing to wear, and if I return safely to my father's house, then the LORD will be my God.'"
Genesis 28:20-21

In the meantime, Scripture counsels patience while the suffering continues for a while longer. We don't like this kind of advice today. We want solutions to our problems now! As Christians we are certain that God will ultimately remove all suffering (see Rev. 7:15-17; 21:3-4), but in the interim we are often reluctant to wait.

Unfortunately, some people have used God's assurance of future relief to justify passive acceptance or resignation about present suffering. Belief in the ultimate end of all suffering doesn't relieve us of our responsibility to try to alleviate suffering here and now.

This study will use God's Word to correct these misunderstandings as we identify ways God cares for us in our suffering and promises to help us.

The account of the three Hebrew men in the fiery furnace has introduced the biblical themes of God's power, compassion, and comfort in relation to evil and suffering. Did you notice the men's confidence? Even if God chose not to miraculously deliver them, they seemed to have no doubts, reservations, or perplexities. When you and I suffer, we usually have lots of questions. In our study we will need to explore the biblical witness to both the questions and the answers about suffering.

In this life we will never have a totally rational answer to the question of why we suffer. We are not forced, however, to the other extreme of unquestioning resignation. Suffering is indeed ultimately a mystery, but people of faith have some answers. One author suggests that the Bible deals with suffering on two levels: the intellectual level and the survival level.[5] The intellectual level deals with the why question: why do I suffer? The survival level deals with a practical response to suffering. The woman who wrote "Dear Abby" rejected the view that her son was killed for a reason. Too often Christians try to comfort people strictly on an intellectual level, when compassionate ministry requires a survival response.

"Look! God's dwelling is with men, and He will live with them. They will be His people, and God Himself will be with them and be their God. He will wipe away every tear from their eyes Death will exist no longer; grief, crying, and pain will exist no longer, because the previous things have passed away."
Revelation 21:3-4

21. Identify the following actions as intellectual *(I)* or survival *(S)* responses to suffering.

____ **a. Listening**
____ **b. Discussing why God allows suffering**
____ **c. Sending a card**
____ **d. Sharing Bible verses about God's compassion and concern**

You probably recognized that statements *a*, *c*, and *d* are survival responses to suffering.

Although Shadrach, Meshach, and Abednego may seem too optimistic for some of us, they were aware of what I like to call the omnicompetence of God. Not only is God able to help us (omnipotence) and willing to help us (omnibenevolence), but He also does help us in all situations (omnicompetence).[6] Probably the most widely quoted biblical passage on suffering is Romans 8:28.

Omnicompetence
God's ability to help people in all situations

"We know that in all things God works for the good of those who love him, who have been called according to his purpose."
Romans 8:28, NIV

22. Read that verse in the margin. Check the correct statement.
☐ **Paul said everything that happens is good.**
☐ **Paul said in all things God works for good.**

Identify a struggle with evil or suffering that you are experiencing: _____

Do you believe that God *can* bring good from any bad situation?
☐ **Yes** ☐ **No** **Do you believe that God *will* bring good from every bad situation?** ☐ **Yes** ☐ **No**

Paul was not suggesting that everything that happens is good but that in all things, good or bad, God can and does work for the good. Divine omnicompetence means that no situation is beyond God's ultimate control or help. God does not cause the suffering in all cases, but He can help us in every situation. In the chapters that follow, we will explore in more depth the biblical writers' understanding of God's relationship to human suffering.

---

[1] E. S. Gerstenberger and W. Schrage, *Suffering*, trans. John E. Steely (Nashville: Abingdon, 1980), 22–102, 140–64.

[2] C. S. Lewis, *The Problem of Pain* (New York: Macmillan, 1944), 89.

[3] "After the Tsunami: Rebuilding Lives and Restoring Hope" [online, cited 15 April 2005]. Available on the Internet: *www.samaritan'spurse.org/index.asp?section=Projects&page=projects_news_122704.txt*.

[4] Warren McWilliams, *Free in Christ: The New Testament Understanding of Freedom* (Nashville: Broadman Press, 1984), 20.

[5] Daniel J. Simundson, *Faith Under Fire: Biblical Interpretations of Suffering* (Minneapolis: Augsburg, 1980), 15–16.

[6] Donald G. Bloesch, *Essentials of Evangelical Theology*, vol. 1 (San Francisco: Harper & Row, 1978), 28.

Chapter 2

God Is Compassionate

Suffering in the Pentateuch

A FEW YEARS AGO ONE OF MY BEST FRIENDS, Dick Rader, died of cancer at an early age. He and his wife, Sue, had served for several years as missionaries in Africa, but they had returned to the States because of Sue's poor health. Although God miraculously healed Sue, she experienced additional health problems over the next several years. In time Dick was diagnosed with colon cancer that had spread to his liver. Treatments were unsuccessful, and Dick died after a 10-month battle. I'll never forget Dick's memorial service, which was held in our university chapel. His family and friends highlighted both the tragedy of his untimely death and the joy of a life lived well for the cause of Christ. Despite our sorrow over Dick's passing, we knew he had accomplished a great deal for God's kingdom. Dick and Sue always found joy in living for Christ, even while suffering severe health problems.

Pentateuch
*The first five books
of the Hebrew Bible—
Genesis, Exodus,
Leviticus, Numbers,
and Deuteronomy*

"God said, 'Let Us
make man in Our
image, according to
Our likeness. They will
rule the fish of the sea,
the birds of the sky, the
animals, all the earth,
and the creatures that
crawl on the earth.'
So God created man
  in His own image;
He created him in
  the image of God;
He created them male
  and female."
Genesis 1:26-27

"God blessed them, and
God said to them, 'Be
fruitful, multiply, fill
the earth, and subdue
it. Rule the fish of the
sea, the birds of the sky,
and every creature that
crawls on the earth.'
God saw all that He
had made, and it was
very good."
Genesis 1:26-28,31

Like Dick and Sue, everyone has a life story that includes both tragedy and joy. The Bible is also a story—the true story of God's dealings with humankind. That story too is a mixture of tragedy and joy. Because the story is so long and complex, we will discuss the biblical view of suffering by examining major blocks of the Bible and by highlighting key events and teachings. In this chapter we will discover truths the Hebrews learned about suffering through the experiences recorded in the first five books of the Hebrew Bible, the Pentateuch.

A Spoiled World

Humanity's history with suffering begins in Genesis. God created a good world, but sin introduced evil and suffering into it.

Genesis 1–2 describes God's good creation. When God looked at the world He had created, He evaluated it as "very good" (Gen. 1:31). Pain and suffering were not part of His original creation.

1. Read the verses from Genesis 1 in the margin. What made the creation of humanity good?
☐ **Humanity ruled the earth.**
☐ **Humanity was created in God's image.**
☐ **Humanity was fruitful.**

God's approval included humans, who were made in His image and were given the responsibility of taking care of His creation. Humans were very good, but God also created them with the ability to choose—to obey or disobey His will.

2. Read Genesis 2:16-17 in the margin on page 31. Underline the command God gave Adam and Eve.

Satan appears in Genesis 3 in the guise of a serpent to tempt the original humans, introducing his plan for evil and suffering. In an event traditionally called the fall, Adam and Eve succumbed to Satan's temptation and rebelled against God by eating from the tree God said to avoid. Evil and suffering entered human history through their sin. Adam and Eve were created with finite freedom; they could choose to obey God or to sin against Him. Sadly, they chose disobedience, and a heavy price was exacted—death!

3. Read in the margin the consequences of humanity's initial rebellion in Genesis 3:16-17. Circle the words that indicate pain, suffering, or hardship.

Adam and Eve and all humankind would experience pain and suffering because of this original sin. The decision to rebel against God tarnished the good world He had provided, bringing several tragic consequences to the first couple. The fallout includes their alienation from God and their expulsion from Eden (see Gen. 3:23).[1] Since the fall, all people inherit a sin nature—a natural inclination to sin. In addition, Adam and Eve's sin led to the suffering of the entire created order. Our world is now a fallen world that desperately needs God's help. One theologian put it succinctly: "Creation is fallen under a curse and needs supernatural healing."[2] Humanity and all creation need redemption. They need the Redeemer!

4. Read Romans 8:18-22 in the margin on page 32. Underline descriptions of sin's corruption of the world.

Satan's relationship to our suffering will surface several times in this study. It is important that we understand his role in our suffering, the influence he has in our world, and the limitations God has placed on his activity. Satan can wreak havoc in our lives if we are not aware of his schemes and alert to his presence. Peter warned: "Be sober! Be on the alert! Your adversary the Devil is prowling around like a roaring lion, looking for anyone he can devour. Resist him, firm in the faith, knowing that the same sufferings are being experienced by your brothers in the world" (1 Pet. 5:8-9). Every time we yield to Satan's temptation to sin, we will experience destructive consequences. Those consequences often involve pain and suffering for ourselves and others.

Genesis 4–11 describes the expansion of sin in history. In chapter 4 the first murder occurred when Cain killed Abel. By chapters 6–7 humanity had become so wicked that God sent a flood to cleanse the earth. In Genesis 11 when human sin emerged as arrogance, God dispersed the people who had built the tower of Babel.

Near the end of Genesis 11 we meet Abram, who played a major role in God's redemptive plan for humanity. Genesis 12–50 includes the accounts of our spiritual ancestors. God promised to bless the

"The Lord God commanded the man, 'You are free to eat from any tree of the garden, but you must not eat from the tree of the knowledge of good and evil, for on the day you eat from it, you will certainly die.'"
Genesis 2:16-17

"[God] said to the woman:
'I will intensify your
*   labor pains;*
you will bear children
*   in anguish.*
Your desire will be
*   for your husband,*
yet he will dominate
*   you.'*
And He said to Adam,
'Because you listened
*   to your wife's voice and*
ate from the tree about
*   which I commanded you,*
"Do not eat from it":
The ground is cursed
*   because of you.*
You will eat from it
*   by means of painful*
*   labor*
all the days of your
*   life.'"*
Genesis 3:16-17

"I consider that the sufferings of this present time are not worth comparing with the glory that is going to be revealed to us. For the creation eagerly waits with anticipation for God's sons to be revealed. For the creation was subjected to futility—not willingly, but because of Him who subjected it—in the hope that the creation itself will also be set free from the bondage of corruption into the glorious freedom of God's children. For we know that the whole creation has been groaning together with labor pains until now." Romans 8:18-22

earth through Abram and his descendants (see Gen. 12:2-3). That blessing would come in the person of Jesus, the Redeemer—the ultimate solution to humanity's sin problem.

The first 11 chapters of Genesis set the stage for the biblical account of sin, suffering, and salvation. In them we can identify some foundational truths for our study of evil and suffering:

- God created a good world.
- Humans were created in God's image and were entrusted with the responsibility of caring for God's creation.
- God created humans with the capacity to choose obedience or rebellion (sin).
- Humans chose to sin—to rebel against God, unleashing much suffering into human history.
- Satan tempted the first humans to sin and continues to tempt us today. Because we also have the choice of obedience, we can resist the enemy's temptations.
- Sin has terrible consequences, including our inherited sin nature, our alienation from God and other people, and the corruption of the natural world.
- A Savior is foreshadowed who will ultimately defeat sin, death, and suffering.

5. To check your understanding, indicate whether these statements are true (T) or false (F).

____ a. The first humans created were good.

____ b. Everything God created was good.

____ c. Satan is the cause of evil in the world.

____ d. Sin is more an action than an attitude.

____ e. When we sin, we are in a state of rebellion.

____ f. Sin is a choice.

____ g. Since the fall, humans inherit a sin nature.

____ h. Suffering exists because evil exists.

____ i. We can sin without experiencing consequences.

Did you have trouble with any of these? Here are the correct answers: a. T, b. T, c. F (Sin is the cause of evil in the world.), d. F (Sin begins with our attitudes or thoughts and is manifested in our actions; therefore, we can sin in thought alone.), e. T, f. T (Satan cannot make us sin; he can tempt us, but he does not have the power to make us rebel.), g. T, h. T (We now live in a fallen, evil world, so even innocent suffering exists because of our fallen state.), i. F (All sin has consequences, whether they are physical or spiritual, present or future, known or unknown.).

Suffering and God's Sovereignty

"God is great; God is good," a familiar mealtime prayer begins. Those words also characterize the Hebrews' experience of God. Although the Hebrews frequently suffered, they almost always turned to God as a great and good Deity. Joseph's story, beginning in Genesis 37, highlights this Hebrew understanding. Joseph had been sold into Egyptian slavery by his brothers, falsely accused of attempted rape, imprisoned for two years, and confronted with the challenge of providing food for the Egyptians during a seven-year famine. Yet through all he endured, Joseph still saw God as good.

**6. Read Genesis 45:4-8 in the margin. What was Joseph's attitude toward his brothers? ☐ Angry ☐ Worried ☐ Forgiving
What role did Joseph think God had in his slavery experience?
☐ A direct role ☐ An indirect role ☐ No role at all
What was God's ultimate purpose for Joseph?
☐ To be pharaoh ☐ To save lives
☐ To take revenge on his brothers**

When he met his brothers in Egypt, Joseph did not seek revenge. Instead, he forgave them, consoled them, and reassured them that God intended for Joseph to be in Egypt from the beginning. Later in the account Joseph told his brothers, " 'You planned evil against me; God planned it for good' " (Gen. 50:20). Joseph's suffering had a purpose. God strategically positioned Joseph to use his administrative ability to enable the Egyptians, as well as his own family, to escape the famine's worst consequences. His intervention preserved the nation of Israel.

Because Joseph was convinced of God's sovereignty, he was not at all puzzled about why the famine occurred. He had earlier explained to Pharaoh that the famine was something God was about to do (see Gen. 41:25,28,32). Joseph and most Hebrews did not have a problem reconciling natural suffering and God's goodness. The typical Hebrew viewed God as the ultimate explanation

"Joseph said to his brothers, 'Please, come near me,' and they came near. 'I am Joseph, your brother,' he said, 'the one you sold into Egypt. And now don't be worried or angry with yourselves for selling me here, because God sent me ahead of you to preserve life. For the famine has been in the land these two years, and there will be five more years without plowing or harvesting. God sent me ahead of you to establish you as a remnant within the land and to keep you alive by a great deliverance. Therefore it was not you who sent me here, but God.' "
Genesis 45:4-8

Sovereignty
God's unlimited rule over His creation

" 'Because the dream was given twice to Pharaoh, it means that the matter has been determined by God, and He will soon carry it out.' "
Genesis 41:32

of all events. "In the beginning God" (Gen. 1:1) was an adequate perspective for viewing all of life's problems.

To believers today, such a perspective might seem naïve or even dangerously deterministic, but the Hebrews' main concern was to affirm God's centrality to their faith. Although the Pentateuch does not wrestle with some of the tough intellectual problems of our day, it affirms God's greatness and goodness in all situations. Also, the Hebrews were not concerned with distinguishing between primary and secondary causes of events. For instance, whether a woman could conceive a child was attributed to God's intervention, not to the act of sexual intercourse (for example, see Gen. 4:1; 29:31). Because God was the Creator and Governor of the universe, the Hebrews rarely saw a need to distinguish between His responsibility for an event and a secondary or intermediary cause. As we saw in chapter 1, however, the danger associated with this view is that God is sometimes blamed for everything that happens.

7. Check the two ways God's sovereignty affected the Hebrews' view of natural suffering.
☐ **They didn't distinguish between primary and secondary causes.**
☐ **They weren't convinced of God's goodness.**
☐ **They saw nature as operating independently of God's influence.**
☐ **They saw God's sovereignty as an adequate explanation.**

The Hebrews accepted God's sovereignty as an acceptable explanation of natural suffering; therefore, they didn't distinguish between primary and secondary causes of suffering. Occasionally, Hebrew writers mentioned that God works in and through nature or human activity. For example, working through nature, God provided the dry ground for the Hebrews to cross through the sea as they fled from Egypt by causing a strong wind to blow "all that night" (Ex. 14:21) and hold back the water.

An example of God's sovereignty interacting with human activity is the hardening of Pharaoh's heart.

" 'I [God] will harden Pharaoh's heart so that he will pursue them. Then I will receive glory by means of Pharaoh and all his army, and the Egyptians will know that I am the LORD.' "
Exodus 14:4

8. Read Exodus 14:4 in the margin. Who appears to be responsible for Pharaoh's hardened heart?
☐ **Pharaoh**   ☐ **Moses**   ☐ **God**

At first glance it seems that God punished the Egyptian leader and his people for doing something God forced Pharaoh to do. That's not fair, we argue. However, previous passages describing Pharaoh's heart contain no reference to God's hardening Pharaoh. Pharaoh was stubborn by his own choice.

9. Read the Scriptures in the margin and note the progression of Pharaoh's hardness of heart. Then answer these questions. How did Pharaoh's heart condition begin (see Ex. 5:2)?
☐ **With disbelief and rebellion**
☐ **With callousness toward the Israelites**
☐ **With a curse by his sorcerers**

What effect did Moses' signs have on Pharaoh's heart (see Ex. 7:10-13)? Pharaoh was—
☐ **amazed;**
☐ **unimpressed because his sorcerer's could replicate them;**
☐ **angered and humiliated.**

What word did God use in Exodus 7:14 to describe the precondition of Pharaoh's heart? _____

In Exodus 8:15 who was responsible for Pharaoh's heart condition? ☐ **Pharaoh himself** ☐ **God**

After the sixth plague (see Ex. 9:12, p. 36) we see that God—
☐ **intervened to soften Pharaoh's heart;**
☐ **hardened an already hardened heart;**
☐ **ignored Pharaoh's heart and moved around him to accomplish His purpose.**

Look back at Exodus 14:4 in the margin on page 34. Underline the words that indicate God's purpose in further hardening Pharaoh's already rebellious heart.

Determined to hold on to his labor force, Pharaoh would naturally have been opposed to the Hebrews' leaving Egypt. God's hardening of Pharaoh's heart intensified or confirmed his resistance.[3] God knew the condition of Pharaoh's heart all along and had informed

"Pharaoh responded, 'Who is the Lord that I should obey Him by letting Israel go? I do not know the Lord, and what's more, I will not let Israel go.'"
Exodus 5:2

"Aaron threw down his staff before Pharaoh and his officials, and it became a serpent. But then Pharaoh called the wise men and sorcerers—the magicians of Egypt, and they also did the same thing by their occult practices. ... Pharaoh's heart hardened, and he did not listen to them, as the Lord had said."
Exodus 7:10-13

"Then the Lord said to Moses, 'Pharaoh's heart is unyielding; he refuses to let the people go.'"
Exodus 7:14, NIV

"When Pharaoh saw that there was relief, he hardened his heart and would not listen to them, as the Lord had said."
Exodus 8:15

"The LORD hardened Pharaoh's heart and he did not listen to them, as the LORD had told Moses."
Exodus 9:12

Monotheism
Belief in and worship of one God

Polytheism
Belief in and worship of many gods

Moses that Pharaoh would resist his demands. God did not make a hard heart from a soft, obedient one. He simply allowed the natural hardening process of rebellion to occur in order to display His glory.

The Hebrew emphasis on God as the primary, or even sole, cause of events should be set in the context of the ancient world. We have seen that the Hebrews firmly believed that God is ultimately in control of all things. Given this conviction, any reference to natural or human causation might seem to threaten God's unique authority. The Hebrews were often a small island of monotheists in an ocean of polytheists. They probably saw their liberation from Egypt, for example, as a contest between the true God, Yahweh, and the Egyptian deities who claimed to control the forces of nature.

This thinking lies behind the Pentateuch's frequent emphasis on God's uniqueness. At the burning bush when Moses protested that he could not speak for God because of a lack of eloquence, God responded: "'Who made the human mouth? Who makes him mute or deaf, seeing or blind? Is it not I, the LORD?'" (Ex. 4:11).

10. Check the correct interpretation of God's response.
☐ **God was explaining why physical disabilities exist.**
☐ **God was emphasizing His sufficiency for Moses' need.**

To interpret such a passage as God's response to our questions about the origin of physical disabilities is unfair. God was not explaining why the blind and lame were born that way. He was responding to Moses' excuses for not returning to Egypt to demand the Hebrews' liberation. God is not the author of evil, but in our fallen, spoiled world, physical handicaps occur. When sin entered the world, so did sickness, suffering, and pain—the far-reaching, inevitable consequences of humanity's choosing rebellion over God's plan.

11. How does your belief in God's sovereignty affect your view of suffering?

_____

_____

_____

Suffering and Punishment

If God is great and good, why do evil and suffering exist? The Hebrews recognized that much suffering is a punishment for sin. Indeed, the most common explanation for suffering in the Old Testament is probably that people suffer because they deserve it. This view, which scholars often call the doctrine of retribution, is a major theme throughout both testaments. In its most basic form the doctrine of retribution can pictured this way:

Bad ➔ suffering   **Good ➔ success**

In recent years the trials and convictions of several prominent business leaders have illustrated the truth of the doctrine of retribution. Corporate scandals have frequently made the news, and some business executives have suffered the consequences of their illegal and immoral actions. The doctrine of retribution is based on several fundamental Hebrew convictions, including God's justice, human freedom, and human responsibility. Let's return to the opening chapters of Genesis to more closely examine the direct relationship between suffering and punishment.

12. Read the account of the fall in the margins on pages 37–38. Check the point at which you think sin occurred.
☐ **When Satan initiated the conversation**
☐ **When Eve responded to the serpent**
☐ **When Eve chose to believe the fruit was good**
☐ **When Eve took the bite of the forbidden fruit**

Adam and Eve were free to live in communion with God, but they chose to disobey Him. The serpent's questions did not cause their sin, and certainly God did not cause their disobedience. Eve chose to sin. Notice that her response to Satan in verse 3 was a subtle distortion of God's word. In Genesis 2:17 the only restriction God had placed on Adam and Eve was to avoid eating the forbidden fruit. Eve lied when she added that they were not to touch it. Satan distracted Eve by casting doubt on God's command, and Eve's reply shows that she was on a slippery decline. Her sin occurred before the act of eating the forbidden fruit. Sin began with her attitude of rebellion, choosing to desire the fruit God forbade. Her sin took

Doctrine of Retribution
The view that actions have consequences

"Now the serpent [Satan] was the most cunning of all the wild animals that the LORD *God had made. He said to the woman, 'Did God really say, "You can't eat from any tree in the garden"?' The woman said to the serpent, 'We may eat the fruit from the trees in the garden. But about the fruit of the tree in the middle of the garden, God said, "You must not eat it or touch it, or you will die."' 'No! You will not die,' the serpent said to the woman. 'In fact, God knows that when you eat it your eyes will be opened and you will be like God, knowing good and evil.' Then the woman saw that the tree was good for food and delightful to look at, and that it was desirable for obtaining wisdom. So she took some of its fruit and ate it; she also gave some to her husband, who was with her, and he ate it.*

Then the eyes of both of them were opened, and they knew they were naked; so they sewed fig leaves together and made loincloths for themselves."
Genesis 3:1-7

"The LORD said to Moses and Aaron, 'Because you did not trust Me to show My holiness in the sight of the Israelites, you will not bring this assembly into the land I have given them.'"
Numbers 20:12

"They set out from Mount Hor by way of the Red Sea to bypass the land of Edom, but the people became impatient because of the journey. The people spoke against God and Moses: 'Why have you led us up from Egypt to die in the wilderness? There is no bread or water, and we detest this wretched food!' Then the LORD sent poisonous snakes among the people, and they bit them so that many Israelites died."
Numbers 21:4-6

root when she chose to believe Satan's lie that the fruit was good instead of heeding God's warning that the fruit of the tree would bring spiritual and physical death. When Eve tasted the fruit, she was acting from the sin that was already in her heart.

Although we can't explain all human suffering as a direct result of sin, the root of sin is rebellion, and rebellion always results in suffering, separation from God, and pain. Adam and Eve were punished for their sin, and their rebellion still causes suffering today. Evil and suffering are connected to humans' rebellious choices.

Several episodes in the Exodus experience illustrate the retributive principle. When the people sinned, God punished them.

13. Examine the two passages from Numbers in the margin. In Numbers 20:12 what did Moses fail to do?
☐ **Trust God**   ☐ **Show God's holiness**   ☐ **Claim the land**
What was his punishment? _____

In Numbers 21:4-6 how did the people sin? Check all that apply.
☐ **They became impatient.**
☐ **They spoke against God and detested what He had given them.**
☐ **They wanted to die.**

What consequence resulted from their rebellion?

_____

The 40 years the Hebrews spent in the wilderness clearly illustrate the retributive principle. After receiving the laws at Mount Sinai, Moses and the people marched to Kadesh, near the promised land. Twelve Hebrew spies spent 40 days on a reconnaissance trip to Canaan, the land God had promised the Hebrews. The majority report was that Canaan was too strong to conquer, but Joshua and Caleb encouraged an invasion (see Num. 13:30). However, the Hebrews did not listen to the minority report. God punished their unfaithfulness by pronouncing that they would wander for 40 years in the wilderness before the next generation could enter the promised land (see Num. 14:26-35). On many occasions during that period the Hebrews received God's retributive punishment for their disobedience. When Korah and his followers rebelled against

Moses, they were killed (see Num. 16:31-35). Several times the people complained and were punished. Even Moses was excluded from entering Canaan because of his disobedience. These experiences demonstrate that God sent suffering as a punishment for sin. In each instance sin was manifested in the people's choices to rebel against God, to elevate their desires or plans above His commands. And they suffered. The suffering came from a just God who had created free people who were accountable to Him for their actions.

Several laws in the Pentateuch also reflect the retributive principle. A Hebrew who obeyed God's laws would prosper, but one who disobeyed would be punished. A clear example of this principle is the law that later scholars called *lex talionis* (law of retaliation): "'If there is an injury, then you must give life for life, eye for eye, tooth for tooth, hand for hand, foot for foot, burn for burn, bruise for bruise, wound for wound'" (Ex. 21:23-25). The *lex talionis* established the principle that punishment should be as severe as the sin.

Lex Talionis
The law of retaliation set forth in Exodus 21:23-25

The Hebrew law often distinguished between two basic types of people. The Holiness Code (see Lev. 17–26) presented two ways of life and their consequences. Those who obeyed God would prosper, and the disobedient would suffer. The rewards and punishments were specific: rain, good harvests, peace, military victory, large families, and God's presence for the obedient (see Lev. 26:3-13); disease, famine, military defeat, God's absence, and much more for the disobedient (see Lev. 26:14-39). Moses frequently made this comparison in Deuteronomy as he reviewed God's dealings with the Hebrews and prepared them for the conquest of Canaan (see Deut. 11:13-17,26-28). In his last major address before his death, Moses returned to the retribution theme: "'See, today I have set before you life and prosperity, death and adversity'" (Deut. 30:15). The choices were clear, and so were the consequences of those choices.

14. Match the terms with their meanings.

____ 1. Doctrine of retribution   a. Actions have consequences.

____ 2. *Lex talionis*   b. Two contrasting ways of life that bring rewards or punishments

____ 3. Holiness Code   c. Punishment should match the severity of the sin.

"The LORD's anger burned against them, and He left. As the cloud moved away from the tent, Miriam's skin suddenly became diseased, as white as snow. When Aaron turned toward her, he saw that she was diseased and said to Moses, 'My lord, please don't hold against us this sin we have so foolishly committed.'"
Numbers 12:9-10

"I the LORD thy God am a jealous God, visiting the iniquity of the fathers upon the children unto the third and fourth generation of them that hate me; and shewing mercy unto thousands of them that love me, and keep my commandments."
Exodus 20:5-6, KJV

Although the principle of retribution explains numerous examples of suffering throughout the Bible, we can detect significant differences in the interpretation of this theme. In the Pentateuch we can identify three aspects of retribution.

Retribution in the Pentateuch usually involves God's relation to groups rather than individuals. The Pentateuch doesn't ignore individuals' actions. An example of individual retribution is seen in Miriam's rebellion against God's chosen leader, Moses, and the immediate consequence of her leprosy (see Num. 12:9-10). But most of the discussion in the Pentateuch focuses on the obedience or disobedience of the entire family, tribe, or nation. Scholars suggest that early in Hebrew history the sense of interdependence within social units was so strong that the sense of individual responsibility was seldom highlighted. The Hebrews had a stronger sense of corporate personality than we have in our individualistic society. Some passages in the Pentateuch indicate that this group solidarity crossed generations. The fathers' iniquity, which means moral crookedness or an immoral behavior pattern, would cause suffering for the children as they developed the same habits and behaviors as their parents (see Ex. 20:5-6; 34:7).

15. Name iniquities—immoral behavior patterns—that have long-lasting consequences, extending to other family members or future generations.

Today we see that children often develop habits and values similar to those of their parents. Later Hebrews would accent individual responsibility, but the Hebrews never totally deserted this sense of corporate responsibility. Although a simplistic development from corporate to individual accountability in Hebrew history cannot be traced, the emphasis had clearly shifted by the time of Jeremiah and Ezekiel (for example, see Jer. 31:29-30; Ezek. 18).

Retribution in the Pentateuch usually involves rewards and punishments experienced in this life. In the Pentateuch the rewards for obedience include such examples as health, long life, wealth, large families, and military success. Early in their history the Hebrews did not have a well-developed view of the afterlife. The dead, good and bad, went to a shadowy place known as Sheol, the underworld (see Gen. 37:35; Num. 16:33). The view that rewards and punishments would continue past death was not clear to the Hebrews. This life was what counted, and God would deal with people in the here and now. In their early history the Hebrews repeatedly needed to be reminded to rely on God for their basic existence. The fact that God provided essentials such as food, clothing, and shelter helped correct a sense of self-sufficiency or an attraction to the nature gods worshiped in Canaan (see Deut. 8:11-20).

Retribution in the Pentateuch frequently comes directly from God. Although actions may have built-in consequences, some passages in the Pentateuch indicate that God directly causes rewards and punishments. For example, God dealt directly with Adam, Eve, and Cain. When Onan refused to practice levirate marriage with Tamar, God killed him (see Gen. 38:7-10). Miriam's leprosy was direct punishment for her criticism of Moses' marriage (see Num. 12:9-10). Korah and his followers were punished for rebelling against Moses (see Num. 16). God sent fiery serpents to punish the Israelites when they complained about the hardships of the wilderness period (see Num. 21:4-9).

Levirate Marriage
The practice of a man's marrying his dead brother's widow and fathering an heir for his brother

**16. How do you react to the principle of retribution?
Mark the following *agree* or *disagree*.**

	AGREE	DISAGREE
The doctrine of retribution operates today.	☐	☐
Retribution primarily affects groups.	☐	☐
Retribution primarily affects individuals.	☐	☐
Retribution extends to subsequent generations.	☐	☐
Retribution primarily applies to this life.	☐	☐
Retribution comes directly from God.	☐	☐
Retribution explains all suffering.	☐	☐

Most people today recognize the validity of the retributive principle, at least in its basic form. Our actions have consequences. We have seen the ripple effect of our actions having consequences we never envisioned or intended. Retribution can serve as an explanation of much of the suffering we experience. A life lived in compliance with God's will is often more meaningful and prosperous than one lived outside that will.

We also need to recognize, however, that the doctrine of retribution as developed in the Pentateuch is not the Bible's final word on suffering. When we use the retributive principle as the exclusive explanation of suffering, we ignore much that the Bible has to teach us on the subject. As we explore other parts of Scripture, we will see several other themes and principles that will illuminate the cause of our suffering.

Suffering and God's Compassion

If God related to us strictly on the basis of retribution, we would probably see Him as a celestial Santa Claus, checking His list to see who is naughty and nice. Fortunately, the Bible reveals God as having many attributes beyond justice. Although the Hebrews generally told stories about God's actions in history, they occasionally gave brief sketches of His character. For example, "Yahweh—Yahweh is a compassionate and gracious God, slow to anger and rich in faithful love and truth, maintaining faithful love to a thousand generations, forgiving wrongdoing, rebellion, and sin" (Ex. 34:6-7). God identified with the Hebrews in their suffering and actively involved Himself in relieving it.

Although the theme of God's involvement is clear throughout the Pentateuch, perhaps the clearest example is the Exodus, the greatest event in Hebrew history. The Hebrews had migrated to Egypt to join Joseph and to escape seven years of famine. Then the Egyptian leadership changed and enslaved the Hebrews.

God was aware of His people's situation: "The Israelites groaned because of their difficult labor, and they cried out; and their cry for help ascended to God because of the difficult labor. God saw the Israelites, and He took notice" (Ex. 2:23,25). God chose to help relieve their suffering by using Moses as their leader.

"The LORD said, 'I have observed the misery of My people in Egypt, and have heard them crying out because of their oppressors, and I know about their sufferings. I have come down to rescue them from the power of the Egyptians and to bring them from that land to a good and spacious land, a land flowing with milk and honey.'"
Exodus 3:7-8

17. Read in the margin God's words to Moses in Exodus 3:7-8. God interacted with His people's suffering in the five ways on the following page. Describe how God acts in your life in the same ways. Look up the other Scriptures for additional insight. An example is provided.

a. God observed the misery of His people. *God's eye is always* *on me; He sees everything that happens to me* **(see Ps. 33:13-14).**

b. God heard them crying out. _____

_____**(see 1 John 5:14-15).**

c. God knew about their suffering. _____

_____**(see Ps. 139:2-4).**

d. God came down to rescue them from the power of their enemy. _____

_____**(see John 6:38-39).**

e. God delivered them and gave them safe passage from their troubles. _____

_____**(see Ps. 34:17-18).**

This pattern of identification and involvement is essential to the biblical portrait of God. In fact, God's action in the Exodus experience is so fundamental to Hebrew thought that whenever the Hebrews suffered, they expected a new Exodus. Later in Hebrew history, if God did not immediately respond to a crisis, the people were perplexed by His apparent disregard of their plight.[4]

18. Examine the list of life crises below. Check any you have experienced. Underline any that made you feel disconnected from God's help.

☐ **Joblessness**   ☐ **Financial burdens**   ☐ **Abuse**
☐ **Illness**   ☐ **Relocation decisions**   ☐ **Grief**
☐ **Grief**   ☐ **Unfaithful spouse**   ☐ **Natural disaster**
☐ **Persecution**   ☐ **Wayward child**   ☐ **Homelessness**
☐ **Divorce**   ☐ **Physical disability**   ☐ **Depression**

Scripture testifies that God sees and knows and cares about any crisis we encounter. God may not respond to our dilemma when we would like or in the way we would like, but He always responds. God may not remove our suffering, but He responds with compassion by strengthening us and enabling us to endure.

    Even in the legal sections of the Pentateuch where the retribution theme is prominent, God's compassion is evident. So that the Hebrews would not fear that God would desert them for a single violation, He reminded them of His willingness to give them a second chance: " 'You will search for the LORD your God, and you will

God sees and knows and cares about any crisis we encounter.

find Him when you seek Him with all your heart and all your soul. When you are in distress and all these things have happened to you, you will return to the LORD your God in later days and obey Him. He will not leave you, destroy you, or forget the covenant with your fathers that He swore to them by oath, because the LORD your God is a compassionate God'" (Deut. 4:29-31). Indeed, God intended the suffering that resulted from sin to have a disciplinary or instructional value as well as exacting His justice.[5] For this reason the laws are often stated in a conditional form (if ..., then ...) to make the choice clear to God's people: you must choose loyalty or disobedience. Just as a parent's discipline might lead to a closer relationship with a child (see Lev. 26:18-28; Deut. 8:5; 30:1-4), God's punishment for sin can lead His children back to God.

As Moses gave his final address to the Israelites before passing his leadership to Joshua, he forewarned the people about God's punishment for any failure to obey. At the same time, he also painted a beautiful portrait of God's compassionate grace toward those who repent and turn back to Him in obedience.

"'When all these things happen to you—the blessings and curses I have set before you—and you come to your senses while you are in all the nations where the LORD your God has driven you, and you and your children return to the LORD your God and obey Him with all your heart and all your soul by doing everything I am giving you today, then He will restore your fortunes, have compassion on you, and gather you again from all the peoples where the LORD your God has scattered you. Even if your exiles are at the ends of the earth, He will gather you and bring you back from there.'"
Deuteronomy 30:1-4

19. Read Deuteronomy 30:1-4 in the margin. What three things was God willing to do for His repentant people?
a. He would _____ their fortunes.
b. He would have _____ on them.
c. He would _____ them from all the places they were scattered.

Read Deuteronomy 8:5 in the margin. Circle the word that describes our relationship with God as He disciplines us.

God's activity in these verses speaks of His loving nature even when He must discipline us. His intent in discipline is to restore, love, and gather us close to Him again. Like children, we can climb into His lap of love and feel His sheltering arms around us.

One of the most intriguing aspects of the Pentateuch's view of God is seen in His decision to relent from exacting punishment that He had earlier decided to carry out. Several times God responded to the penitent pleas of His people and, while still exercising perfect justice, lessened the penalty for their crimes. For instance, God is frequently pictured consulting with the Hebrews about His course

"'Keep in mind that the LORD your God has been disciplining you just as a man disciplines his son.'"
Deuteronomy 8:5

of action.[6] When the Hebrews made the golden calf, God was ready to slay them for their idolatry. Moses interceded with God, asking Him not to destroy all of the people, and "the LORD changed His mind about the disaster He said He would bring on His people" (Ex. 32:14). Eventually, God sent punishment to the Hebrews (see Ex. 32:35) but apparently not as severe as He originally intended.

God's mercy reminds us that He interacts with us on a personal basis. He is a dynamic, living God rather than a static, lifeless Supreme Being. However, we must not picture God as a capricious, whimsical Deity. He changes His stated course of action not because He is fickle but because He is responsive to our cries for mercy. God is not wishy-washy in the way humans often are (see Num. 23:19). Because God is always compassionate, dynamic, and living, He may relate to us in different ways at different times.

God's compassionate identification with His people includes a dimension of sadness or grief over their actions. When humankind was so sinful that God had to send the flood to allow a new beginning, He was sorrowful over the world (see Gen. 6:5-6). The notion that God suffers grief because of His people's disobedience becomes more pronounced in other parts of the Old Testament. The Hebrews who broke God's laws also broke His heart.

20. Describe how you experienced God's compassion when He—

heard your cry for help: _____

_____

gave you a second chance: _____

_____

disciplined you: _____

_____

Is there any behavior or attitude for which you need God's forgiveness? If so, take time now to repent and receive His grace.

"When the LORD saw that man's wickedness was widespread on the earth and that every scheme his mind thought of was nothing but evil all the time, the LORD regretted that He had made man on the earth, and He was grieved in His heart." Genesis 6:5-6

Caring for Those Who Suffer

As the Hebrews learned about God's concern for them, they also realized that He expected them to be concerned about the suffering around them. God's dealings with their forefather, Abraham, showed that their national destiny was to help relieve the suffering of all humanity.

Contemporary readers of the Old Testament often omit the legal sections just as we skim the lengthy genealogies. Within these laws, however, we can find God's instructions for alleviating some human suffering. Although God sometimes miraculously intervened to correct injustice, He often worked through His people. He expected the Hebrews to share His concern for suffering.

The Hebrew law has a strong humanitarian dimension. Because the Hebrews had been enslaved and powerless, they should be especially willing to help the oppressed.

"'Do not deny justice to a foreign resident or fatherless child, and do not take a widow's garment as security. Remember that you were a slave in Egypt, and the LORD *your God redeemed you from there. Therefore I am commanding you to do this.'"*
Deuteronomy 24:17-18

21. Read Deuteronomy 24:17-18 in the margin. What three groups are named?

_____

Hebrew law often highlighted several groups that needed special protection: foreigners, orphans, and widows. Some of the most charitable acts in the Old Testament apply to these minorities. Because the Hebrews had lived in Egypt for several hundred years, they well knew the potential dangers of being foreigners, or resident aliens. The Hebrews should care for them (see Ex. 22:21; 23:9). Orphans and widows were also potentially vulnerable in a patriarchal, male-dominated society, so the Hebrews were frequently reminded to care for those groups (see Ex. 22:22-24; Deut. 10:18).

If a Hebrew lent money to a poor person, he should not charge interest or hold his garment as collateral. If a creditor mistreated a debtor, God would respond: "'If he cries out to Me, I will listen because I am compassionate'" (Ex. 22:27). God expected the Hebrews' conduct and character to reflect His own. Because He is compassionate, His people should be compassionate as well.

God also established special events, the sabbatical year and the jubilee year, when property returned to its original owner and slaves were liberated (see Lev. 25). If the Hebrews had regularly practiced these observances, the economic injustice criticized by later prophets would have been less frequent. The tithe was required not only to support the religious leaders but also to provide resources for the poor and powerless (see Deut. 14:28-29; 26:12-15). The Hebrews realized that poverty would be a perennial problem, and God reminded them that this fact should lead to ongoing concern for the poor, not resignation (see Deut. 15:11). One of God's reasons for establishing the observance of the sabbath was to allow a time of rest for workers and animals (see Ex. 23:12).

22. Read Deuteronomy 27:19 in the margin. Circle the consequence for denying the right to justice and fair treatment.

Why do you think God felt so strongly about these injustices?

_____

How do you think God's command for the Israelites to show compassion would solidify their identity as His people before the pagan world?

_____

"'There will never cease to be poor people in the land; that is why I am commanding you, "You must willingly open your hand to your afflicted and poor brother in your land."'"
Deuteronomy 15:11

"'Cursed is the one who denies justice to a foreign resident, a fatherless child, or a widow.'"
Deuteronomy 27:19

Because God's nature is compassionate and caring, His heart is moved by those who are weak, hurting, neglected, or powerless. When God commanded His people to act in loving and charitable ways to these people groups, He was demanding that they reflect His character before the world. As they did that, pagan nations would see God's character in their lifestyles and would come to know the true God through the Israelites' behavior. Following each command about their behavior and attitudes toward these people, God stated, "'I am the LORD your God.'" He was implying, "You are My people; be like Me." As we interact with our world, we encounter other people groups. Will we reflect God's character in our lifestyles, in our behaviors and attitudes, and in our relationships with those who need a Deliverer?

God expects Christians today to demonstrate the same compassion for orphans, widows, and the poor as the Hebrew law required. In my town several churches have formed a coalition that provides temporary shelter for homeless families. The primary motivation is the compassion that characterizes God. God is concerned about these people, and Christians in Shawnee have found a practical way to minister to the homeless in our community.

23. Beside God's character traits, describe actions you could take that would mirror His character. An example is provided.

GOD'S CHARACTER TRAITS	CHRISTIAN ACTIONS
Compassion for the poor/needy......	*Provide food or material needs*
Mercy	_____
Forgiveness	_____
Patience	_____
Justice	_____

Check one of the actions you will commit to begin.

Lessons from the Pentateuch

We have examined several major views of suffering that will recur throughout the Bible. We can remind ourselves of these themes by looking at the song God gave Moses shortly before Moses' death and the invasion of Canaan. Moses' song in Deuteronomy 32 provided the Hebrews a summary of their experiences with God, especially during the Exodus: they were unfaithful and rebellious; yet God was faithful and changeless, showing mercy and extending compassion. When the Hebrews experienced trouble in the years ahead, they could remember Moses' song: "'When many troubles and afflictions come to them, this song will testify against them, because their descendants will not have forgotten it. For I know what they are prone to do, even before I bring them into the land I swore to given them'" (Deut. 31:21). "If only they were wise" (Deut. 32:29), the Hebrews would learn from these experiences with God. If we are wise, we will also learn the following lessons from the Hebrews' experiences.

Yahweh is the only true God and the One ultimately responsible for the course of human history. The Hebrews would be tempted to follow other gods, but they knew in their hearts that Yahweh alone is real:

God is ultimately responsible for the course of human history.

See now that I alone am He;
there is no God but Me.
I bring death and I give life;
I wound and I heal.
No one can rescue anyone from My hand. Deuteronomy 32:39

God is just in His actions, punishing the sinful and rewarding the faithful.

God is just in His actions, punishing the sinful and rewarding the faithful.

The Rock—His work is perfect;
all His ways are entirely just.
A faithful God, without prejudice,
He is righteous and true. Deuteronomy 32:4

The Hebrews had made a covenant with God at Mount Sinai. God remained faithful to that agreement, but the Hebrews often became fickle, and their actions deserved punishment (see Deut. 32:5-6, 15-33). As we have seen, this doctrine of retribution is a basic explanation of suffering throughout the Bible.

God is loving and compassionate.

The LORD will indeed vindicate His people
and have compassion on His servants
when He sees that their strength is gone
and no one is left—slave or free. Deuteronomy 32:36

Moses' song includes several word pictures for God:
- God is like a father who is deeply concerned about His wayward children (see Deut. 32:5-7).
- God is like an eagle that is teaching its young how to fly (see Deut. 32:11-12).
- God is like a mother who has been rejected by her children (see Deut. 32:18).

The eagle image is especially important because it appears in the background of the covenant at Mount Sinai (see Ex. 19:4-6) and points to a basic pattern in the Bible: God always initiates a relationship with His people through a gracious, loving action such as the Exodus. If the people want to continue that relationship, they enter a covenant with God at His invitation. This pattern is crucial to understanding the Hebrews' early appreciation for the law. The law was not imposed on them by force. They freely agreed to follow God's law in gratitude for their liberation from bondage in Egypt (see Ex. 20:2).

"'I am the LORD *your God, who brought you out of the land of Egypt, out of the place of slavery.'"*
Exodus 20:2

God's basic intention for His people is always good. In Hebrew history when innocent suffering (for example, Joseph's slavery) came from human injustice, God could bring good from it (see Gen. 45:7; 50:20). When God punished His people for their sin, the ultimate goal was that they learned the error of their ways and returned to Him.

God expects His people to be concerned about suffering. God admonished the Hebrews to be especially sensitive to groups such as widows, orphans, foreign residents, and the poor. "'I am compassionate'" (Ex. 22:27) not only describes God's character but also serves as a moral model for Hebrew behavior. To imitate God's character is the basic principle of biblical ethics.

24. On a separate sheet of paper or in the margin, write a prayer affirming the bold headings in "Lessons from the Pentateuch" (pp. 48–50). Pray about God's expectation that you show concern for people who suffer.

---

1 Ted M. Dorman, *A Faith for All Seasons*, 2nd ed. (Nashville: Broadman & Holman, 2001), 127.

2 Roger E. Olson, *The Mosaic of Christian Belief* (Downers Grove, IL: InterVarsity, 2002), 157.

3 Walter C. Kaiser Jr., *Toward Old Testament Ethics* (Grand Rapids, MI: Zondervan, 1983), 252–56.

4 John Bowker, *Problems of Suffering in Religions of the World* (Cambridge: Cambridge University Press, 1970), 7.

5 J. M. Ward, "Discipline, Divine," in *The Interpreter's Dictionary of the Bible*, supplementary volume (Nashville: Abingdon, 1976), 234–36.

6 Terence E. Fretheim, *The Suffering of God: An Old Testament Perspective* (Philadelphia: Fortress, 1984), 49–53.

Chapter 3

How Long, O Lord?
Suffering in the Prophets and the Writings

WHEN SOMETHING BAD HAPPENS, we typically ask, "Why?" That was the national outcry on September 11, 2001, when terrorists flew hijacked airplanes into the twin towers of the World Trade Center and the Pentagon. Thousands were killed or wounded. In the weeks that followed, many Christians wondered why God allowed such evil to occur. Was He punishing America for its sin? Were these events examples of innocent suffering? Was this tragedy an example of God's perfect or permissive will? Was He testing our faith? What role did Satan play in these events? Suddenly, commentators throughout the country were applying almost every biblical view of evil and suffering to the September 11 tragedy.[1]

In this chapter we will deal with biblical teachings on evil and suffering in the second and third divisions of the Hebrew Bible, the Prophets and the Writings. We will discover a wide range of views about evil and suffering in these books, which cover one thousand years of Hebrew history: the conquest of Canaan,

Prophets
A division of Bible books consisting of the Former Prophets (Joshua, Judges, 1–2 Samuel, 1–2 Kings) and the Latter Prophets (Isaiah, Jeremiah, Ezekiel, Hosea, Joel, Amos, Obadiah, Jonah, Micah, Nahum, Habakkuk, Zephaniah, Haggai, Zechariah, Malachi)

Writings
A miscellaneous collection of Bible books consisting of Poetic Books (Job, Psalms, Proverbs); the Festival Scrolls (Ruth, Esther, Ecclesiastes, Song of Songs, Lamentations); and the Historical Books (1–2 Chronicles, Ezra, Nehemiah, Daniel)

the period of the Judges, the united and divided monarchies, the exile, and the reconstruction. Although we will see increasing attention given to innocent suffering in these books, we will encounter themes from the previous chapter: the doctrine of retribution, God's sovereignty, and God's compassion.

Suffering in the Prophets

Throughout their history the Jews have suffered much; yet the Hebrews kept affirming God despite the sorrows they experienced. In the Prophets we will witness some of their suffering, and we will consider what it can teach us about our own trials.

The Cycle of Retribution and Deliverance
The close connection between sin and suffering that we saw in the Pentateuch appears again in the Prophets. Here much Hebrew suffering is also understood as the deserved penalty for sin.

Retribution during the conquest. During the conquest of Canaan, the Hebrews could win battles as long as they remained loyal to God. Their disloyalty, however, led to defeat. At the battle of Jericho, Achan took some spoils of war even though God had clearly prohibited this action (see Deut. 20:16-20). Because of Achan's sin the Hebrews lost the battle at Ai (see Josh. 7:1-2,10-12). Achan and his family were punished for his sin (see Josh. 7:24-26), illustrating the corporate-accountability concept that we observed in the Pentateuch.

Retribution in the period of the judges. Before the Hebrews had a king, the 12 tribes were a loose confederacy or league led by judges. In the Book of Judges a four-step pattern is repeated:

Sin ➜ oppression ➜ repentance ➜ deliverance

Over the years the Hebrews repeatedly rebelled against God, often by following pagan gods. Each time God would punish them, usually by a military threat or oppression from another nation. In response to God's punishment, the people would eventually see the error of their ways and repent. Then God would deliver them through a judge. The pattern is summarized in Judges 2:10-23.

1. Read Judges 2:10-23 in your Bible. What was the primary problem with the new generation (see v. 10)?
☐ **They didn't know their ancestors.** ☐ **They didn't know the Lord.**
How had the Israelites abandoned God?
☐ **They bowed down to other gods.** ☐ **They made God angry.**
The result of their disloyalty was—
☐ **oppression and suffering** ☐ **further corruption** ☐ **both.**

This passage illustrates the pattern of sin that characterized the Hebrew nation during this period. The people did not know the Lord and bowed down to other gods. The results were oppression and suffering. Although God relieved their suffering, the people became more corrupt than their ancestors.

God often used foreign nations as instruments of His discipline. The oppression of God's people by these pagan nations caused Israel to cry out to God for deliverance.

2. Why do you think God disciplined Israel through oppression?
☐ **He wanted them to be subservient to the other nations.**
☐ **He wanted them to turn to Him in obedience.**

God's dealings with His people show that He is more concerned about cultivating our loyalty and obedience to Him than shielding us from all oppression and affliction. Our lifelong faithfulness is far more important than our temporary discomfort.

> Our lifelong faithfulness is far more important than our temporary discomfort.

3. For what national sins do you believe that God will hold Americans accountable?

_____

Do you believe that God is bringing discipline on our nation?
☐ **Yes** ☐ **No**

Retribution in the united monarchy. Numerous events in this period under Kings Saul, David, and Solomon reinforced the idea that suffering comes as people are held accountable for their sin. King Saul's disobedience prompted God to issue several warnings through Samuel (see 1 Sam. 13:13-14) and finally led to his defeat by the Philistines. King David's sin with Bathsheba resulted in the death of their child and several political and domestic problems (see 2 Sam. 12:9-14). Although God gave Solomon superior wisdom, Solomon allowed his foreign wives to lead him into idolatry, and the Hebrew nation split after his death (see 1 Kings 11:4-13).

Retribution in the divided monarchy. Hebrew history in this period was recorded in terms of the retributive principle. The biblical writers normally evaluated kings in terms of their loyalty to God rather than their political or economic success. They attributed the defeat of the Northern Kingdom, Israel, in 722 B.C. to the Hebrews' idolatry and sin (see 2 Kings 17:7-18). The four great eighth-century prophets—Amos, Hosea, Isaiah, and Micah—had each warned the Northern Kingdom of the terrible consequences of disobeying God (see Isa. 1:18-20; Hos. 4:1-5; Amos 2:6-8; Mic. 1:5-9). Apparently, some Hebrews felt that their standing as God's people exempted them from destruction, but the prophets realized that God would reward or punish His children for their actions.

4. Read Hosea 4:1-5. Underline phrases that describe America.

Retribution in the exile. Though the loss of the Northern Kingdom was a harsh blow, the defeat of the Southern Kingdom, Judah, and the exile were probably even more traumatic for the Hebrews.[2] Some thought the south—Jerusalem in particular—was invincible because God had promised David an everlasting house or dynasty (2 Sam. 7:13,16). Although God sent prophets to warn the Hebrews of their actions because "He had compassion on His people" (2 Chron. 36:15), the Babylonian invasion was almost inevitable.

Four prophets—Nahum, Habakkuk, Zephaniah, and Jeremiah—lived during the last days of Judah. Habakkuk was probably the most perplexed about Judah's imminent destruction. Having asked God for help in the face of apparent injustice, Habakkuk was puzzled by God's insistence on bringing the Chaldeans (Babylonians) to punish the Hebrews (see Hab. 1:5-6). The prophet could not readily understand why God would use a bad people to punish a good nation (see Hab. 1:13). Habakkuk never received a neat answer to his quandary. God only assured him that "the righteous one will live by his faith" (Hab. 2:4).

"Hear the word of the
Lord, people of Israel,
for the Lord has a case
against the inhabitants
of the land:
There is no truth,
no faithful love,
and no knowledge
of God in the land!
Cursing, lying, murder,
stealing,
and adultery
are rampant;
one act of bloodshed
follows another.
For this reason
the land mourns,
and everyone who lives
in it languishes,
along with the wild
animals and the
birds of the sky;
even the fish of the sea
disappear.
But let no one dispute;
let no one argue,
for My case is against
you priests.
You will stumble
by day;
the prophet will also
stumble with you
by night.
And I will destroy
your mother."
Hosea 4:1-5

5. Why do you think God sometimes withholds an explanation for our suffering? Check all that apply.
☐ **He wants to keep us in the dark.**
☐ **We would resist His explanation.**
☐ **He wants to build our faith in Him.**
☐ **We don't always need to know why.**

Read Habakkuk 3:17-19 in the margin. Underline the portion that describes what our response to affliction should be, even when we don't understand why we are experiencing it.

Choosing to trust God's sovereignty, Habakkuk concluded his brief book with the assurance that God is in charge of world history even when we don't understand His workings (see Hab. 3:17-19).

If we maintain a close relationship with God during good times, we are able to triumph in who He is and to gain strength from His power when things get difficult. If we wander from Him in times of plenty, we can struggle when we most need His help and comfort. The Hebrews experienced that bitter truth. Their grief during the exile, recorded in Lamentations, is much like that of a lonely widow: "There is no one to offer her comfort" (Lam. 1:2). Their relationship with God was so broken that they perceived Him to be their enemy (see Lam. 3:10-18). They needed a reminder that God is a loving God. Read Lamentations 3:22-23 in the margin.

God did not give up on the Hebrews (see Lam. 3:31-33) even though they deserved the destruction of Jerusalem (see Lam. 1:18). And He will not give up on us today. When we experience isolation from God, it is because we have wandered away. God doesn't move. He continues to invite us into a closer relationship with Him. Sometimes He must use adversity to get our attention!

6. Check God's goals for you.
☐ **Making you happy**
☐ **Deepening your relationship with Him**
☐ **Bring you to greater dependency on Him**
☐ **Making you comfortable**
☐ **Working out His purposes for your life**
☐ **Helping you avoid pain**

"Though the fig tree
does not bud
and there is no fruit
on the vines,
though the olive
crop fails
and the fields
produce no food,
though there are no
sheep in the pen
and no cattle
in the stalls,
yet I will triumph
in the LORD;
I will rejoice in the God
of my salvation!
Yahweh my Lord
is my strength;
He makes my feet
like those of a deer
and enables me to walk
on mountain heights!"
Habakkuk 3:17-19

"Because of the LORD's
faithful love
we do not perish,
for His mercies
never end.
They are new
every morning;
great is Your
faithfulness!"
Lamentations 3:22-23

Identify a time when God used adversity to bring you into a closer relationship with Him.

_____

Innocent Suffering

What do the prophets say about people who suffer even though they haven't rejected God? Although the Hebrew historians and prophets often highlighted national disasters as the consequence of God's punishment, they also recognized that the suffering of smaller groups and individuals was frequently caused by human injustice. Often corrupt Hebrew political, economic, and religious leaders caused innocent suffering by exploiting the poor and needy.

The eighth-century prophets were very concerned about the suffering inflicted by the rich and powerful. Amos, for example, criticized the greed of Israel's leaders (see Amos 2:6-8; 4:1).

"I know your crimes are many and your sins innumerable. They oppress the righteous, take a bribe, and deprive the poor of justice at the gates."
Amos 5:12

7. Read Amos 5:12 in the margin. Underline the three crimes of which the Hebrews were guilty.

What contemporary examples of these practices do you see?

_____

_____

"Let justice flow like water, and righteousness, like an unfailing stream."
Amos 5:24

The Hebrews oppressed the righteous, accepted bribes, and deprived the poor of justice. One of Amos's special targets was arrogant, rich people who led lives of leisure while ignoring the poor and their own imminent doom. "Woe to those who are at ease in Zion" (Amos 6:1), Amos warned, announcing the day of the Lord, when God would punish the wicked (see Amos 5:18-20,24).

Other prophets similarly criticized economic and political injustice (see Hos. 4:8; Isa. 3:13-15; 5:22-23; Mic. 2:1-2; 3:1-3). Jeremiah, for instance, also highlighted the oppression of the poor when he proclaimed Judah's defeat by Babylon. The nation would suffer because of its leaders' unfaithfulness, but many Hebrews had already suffered injustice. Because everyone was greedy (see Jer. 6:13) and people were so callous that they had forgotten how to feel remorse over their sins (see Jer. 6:15; 8:12), many innocent people suffered long before God's judgment fell. Jeremiah urged the Hebrews to concern themselves with aliens, orphans, and widows rather than offer meaningless sacrifices (see Jer. 7:3-7). Jeremiah complimented good King Josiah, who realized that real knowledge of God produced a concern for the disadvantaged (see Jer. 22:16). Through the righteous, God would help the needy.

*"He took up the case
     of the poor and needy,
then it went well.
Is this not what it
     means to know Me?"*
Jeremiah 22:16

Although the doctrine of retribution teaches that some suffering is caused by sin, these prophets remind us that some people suffer innocently. Someone's poverty might result from his laziness, but it might also be caused by unfair labor laws or corrupt employers. The prophets remind us that some suffering is innocent or undeserved, the rich and powerful are held accountable for oppressing the poor, and God will vindicate the poor and needy.

*"Wash the evil from
     your heart, Jerusalem,
so that you will
     be delivered.
How long will
     you harbor
malicious thoughts
     within you?
Your way of life
     and your actions
have brought this
     on you.
This is your punishment.
     It is very bitter,
because it has
     reached your heart!"*
Jeremiah 4:14,18

Individual Responsibility

During the last days of the Southern Kingdom and the exile, Jeremiah and Ezekiel brought a fresh emphasis on personal responsibility, in contrast to the corporate accountability we observed earlier in Hebrew history.

Jeremiah, the weeping prophet, grieved over the message of doom he had to pronounce on Judah as it faced the Babylonian invasion (see Jer. 9:1). The people of Jeremiah's day were very religious, but instead of relying on rituals and external institutions like the temple, the people needed an internal transformation. Read Jeremiah 4:14,18 in the margin.

Jeremiah identified the root of the problem as the heart:

*These people have stubborn and rebellious hearts.
They have turned aside and have gone away.* Jeremiah 5:23

Therefore, Jeremiah pleaded for the people to repent to avoid the Babylonian invasion. Recognizing that personal responsibility is crucial, Jeremiah criticized the popular saying that perpetuated the idea that corporate guilt is transferred across generations: " 'In those days, it will never again be said:

*The fathers have eaten sour grapes,
and the children's teeth are set on edge.*

'Rather, each will die for his own wrongdoing. Anyone who eats sour grapes—his own teeth will be set on edge'" (Jer. 31:29-30).

8. Identify Jeremiah's message for Judah.
☐ **Every individual is responsible to God.**
☐ **Don't indulge in bitter speech.**
☐ **People are responsible for the sins of the previous generation.**

To the Hebrews who felt that their national failure was caused by their ancestors' sins, Jeremiah stressed individual responsibility.

Ezekiel developed this idea even more thoroughly. Like Jeremiah, he recognized that the Hebrews' root problem was internal. God would need to perform a heart transplant to change them: "'I will remove their heart of stone from their bodies and give them a heart of flesh'" (Ezek. 11:19).

Like Jeremiah, Ezekiel built on the earlier recognition of individual responsibility in Hebrew thought (see Deut. 24:16; 2 Kings 14:5-6). Preaching during the exile, Ezekiel challenged the accusation that God is not just: "'Your countrymen say, "The way of the Lord is not just." But it is their way that is not just'" (Ezek. 33:17, NIV). The Hebrews were not sent into exile primarily because of their ancestors' sin. Their own sins were to blame. Merit or guilt would not be transferred across the generations: "'The person who sins is the one who will die'" (Ezek. 18:4). Ezekiel insisted that what each person does individually is what ultimately matters. God is just (see Ezek. 18:25-30). His ultimate desire was for His people to repent and turn to Him (see Ezek. 18:23), but He would judge the good and the bad according to their actions (see Ezek. 18:30).

> What each person does individually is what ultimately matters.

9. Review the national sins you listed on page 53. For which of those do believers have a degree of individual responsibility?

Jeremiah and Ezekiel enrich our study of suffering by focusing attention on personal responsibility. Although our culture publicly espouses the principle of individual accountability, people frequently pass the buck and blame problems on someone or something else, such as parents, government, or society in general. Many factors may influence our decisions and actions, but ultimately, we are responsible and will be held accountable. We cannot exempt ourselves from responsibility by pointing an accusing finger at our parents, our culture, or other influences on us.

10. Identify a family sin that could be broken by an individual who resolves to end the cycle of harmful behavior.

The Hebrews never completely rejected the idea of group accountability, but the Writings (especially Proverbs) and the New Testament frequently emphasize individual responsibility.

Redemptive Suffering

The Prophets introduce a new concept to our understanding of human hurt and God's relationship to it: redemptive suffering. In fact, the deepest insight in the Old Testament on the issue of suffering is the concept of the Suffering Servant in Isaiah's prophecy.[3] Isaiah vividly described the Servant of the Lord who suffered on behalf of others, taking on Himself not only their individual hurts but also the penalty for their sins. To understand this concept of vicarious suffering, we need to place it in two key contexts.

Vicarious Suffering
Suffering in the place of others

The Suffering Servant in the context of the Hebrew view of suffering. The Suffering Servant in the Book of Isaiah represents the third stage in the development of the Hebrew view of suffering:[4]

Stage 1: All sufferers are sinners. This is the concept behind the doctrine of retribution.

Stage 2: Some sufferers are innocent.

Stage 3: Some sufferers are saviors. For a Christian this perspective is intimately linked to the suffering of Jesus Christ.

The Suffering Servant in the context of the history of Judah. Scholars generally agree that Isaiah 40–66 applies to the exile and the liberation of the Hebrews by Cyrus of Persia in 538 B.C. These chapters reflect the idea that Judah had suffered enough and God was setting it free (see Isa. 40:1-2). But even in their freedom, the Hebrews were perplexed by the suffering they had endured.

> " 'Comfort, comfort
>   My people,' says
>   your God.
> Speak tenderly
>   to Jerusalem,
> and announce to her
>   that her time
>   of servitude is over,
> her iniquity
>   has been pardoned,
> and she has received
>   from the
>   LORD's hand
> double for all her sins.' "
> Isaiah 40:1-2

Isaiah comforted the Hebrews with the reminder that all of these events were ultimately caused by God, not another power (see Isa. 41:4; 44:6-8; 45:5-7). Indeed, the emphasis on monotheism in Isaiah 40–66 is probably stronger than anywhere else in the Old Testament. A people who had experienced a lengthy period in a polytheistic culture would have needed this reminder. The Hebrews' defeat by the Babylonians did not mean that God is impotent or uncaring. Rather, God strengthens those who grow weak (see Isa. 40:31) and comforts them.

11. Read Isaiah 43:2 in the margin. What was God's promise to His people?
☐ **He would be with them through their trials.**
☐ **They would have to endure suffering on their own.**

God allows difficulties to happen, but He also sees people through them. He will not ultimately desert them in their trials and their pain. God was much more to the Hebrews than a divine Comforter. He was their Redeemer and Liberator. He delivered them from Babylonian bondage much as He set them free from Egypt in the exodus (see Isa. 43:16-21).

Isaiah's most powerful reassurance, however, came through four songs about the Suffering Servant (see Isa. 42:1-4; 49:1-6; 50:4-11; 52:13–53:12). On one hand, the anonymous servant of the Lord mentioned in these passages sometimes seems to be the Hebrew nation (see Isa. 49:3). God had intended for Israel to be a witness to the other peoples, a "light for the nations" (Isa. 49:6), guiding them to a knowledge of the one true God. On the other hand, several of the servant songs portray an innocent individual, sometimes suffering on behalf of the sinful. These passages clearly anticipate the ministry of Christ. By His suffering He is Savior to both the Hebrews and the world. His suffering was undeserved but redemptive (see Isa. 53:4-5).

12. Read Isaiah 53:4-5 in the margin. Underline the afflictions Christ suffered.

For what crimes was Christ tortured? Circle the words that designate these crimes.

---

*" 'I will be with you
    when you pass
    through the waters,
and when you pass
    through the rivers,
they will not
    overwhelm you.
You will not be scorched
when you walk
    through the fire,
and the flame
    will not burn you.' "*
Isaiah 43:2

*"He Himself bore
    our sicknesses,
and He carried
    our pains;
but we in turn regarded
    Him stricken,
struck down by God,
    and afflicted.
But He was pierced
    because of our
    transgressions,
crushed because
    of our iniquities;
punishment for our
    peace was on Him,
and we are healed
    by His wounds."*
Isaiah 53:4-5

How did Christ's vicarious suffering benefit you? _____

_____

This "man of sorrows" (Isa. 53:3, NIV) suffered and died to pay the penalty for our sin and to bring us peace with God.

13. Stop and thank Jesus for dying for your sin.

God's Justice Will Prevail

Several prophets addressed the Hebrews' trials by emphasizing that the nation's suffering might be eliminated in the future. One day, they taught, good would triumph over evil. Amos, for example, insisted that the sinful would eventually be penalized (see Amos 9:9-10,14). Habakkuk affirmed that God would punish the wicked (see Hab. 3:16). Though some of the wicked thought they could escape God's punishment (see Mal. 3:13-15), Malachi predicted the coming day of the Lord and the arrival of Christ, when justice would prevail (see Mal. 3:1-5; 4:1-5).

Although many prophets had sounded this note of hope through future judgment, the role of the future in the problem of suffering was most frequently accented in apocalyptic literature.[5] The word *apocalyptic* comes from a Greek word meaning *revealing* or *unveiling*. Apocalyptic literature, popularly known for its concern with the future, was usually written against a backdrop of persecution or oppression. Although scholars identify apocalyptic sections in several Old Testament books (see Isa. 24-27; Zech. 9–14), the major example is the Book of Daniel—the account of Daniel and his friends, who were among the Hebrews taken captive in the exile. A primary purpose of apocalyptic literature is to comfort persecuted people by reminding them that eventually God will alleviate their suffering and vindicate them or their cause.

Apocalyptic
Revealing or unveiling. Apocalyptic literature like Daniel and Revelation reflects the persecution of God's people and predicts a future judgment that brings punishment for the wicked and rewards for the faithful.

14. Read Psalm 26:1 in the margin. What gives us assurance of ultimate vindication? Circle your answer.

Knowing that God's justice and timing are perfect, do you consider the goal worth the wait? ☐ Yes ☐ No

"Vindicate me, LORD, because I have lived with integrity and have trusted in the LORD without wavering."
Psalm 26:1

Scripture's emphasis on future deliverance does not guarantee immediate safety. Daniel's three friends were confident that God could save them from the fiery furnace. However, even if no miracle came, they would remain faithful to Him (see Dan. 3:16-18). Apocalyptic literature generally assured readers that "He can rescue us" (Dan. 3:17). It doesn't necessarily specify a time or a method. The apocalyptic emphasis on judgment and justice in the future is a valuable addition to our understanding of evil and suffering.

In time the Hebrews developed a belief in an afterlife that went beyond the shadowy world of the dead, Sheol. A few prophetic passages reflect a growing assurance of life beyond death. The clearest statement of the resurrection of the dead is in Daniel 12:2.

"Many of those who sleep in the dust of the earth will awake, some to eternal life, and some to shame and eternal contempt."
Daniel 12:2

15. Read Daniel 12:2 in the margin, underlining the specific rewards and punishments it mentions.

This assurance that justice will prevail in the future is very meaningful to those who suffer. Counting on God's ultimate triumph over evil, however, doesn't mean we should ignore the suffering around us. Being patient and waiting on the Lord can be combined with responsible Christian action to reduce human suffering. In fact, apocalyptic writers assumed that building confidence in the future, rather than making us accept the status quo, would influence current actions. The stories of Daniel and his friends serve as case studies for living courageously in times of trouble.

16. Identify forms of suffering today that need to be relieved.

_____

Circle one type of suffering that you would like to help alleviate.

God's Compassion for Those Who Suffer

The Prophets also show that God responds to human suffering with compassion. The Prophets frequently describe God as suffering with the Hebrews.[6] Among the earlier prophets, Hosea developed the idea of divine compassion or empathy through beautiful word pictures. God's relation to Israel paralleled Hosea's marriage to Gomer. Just as Gomer had been unfaithful to Hosea, the Hebrews had frequently rebelled against God. Although Israel must suffer for following other lovers (gods), God would woo her back and restore their relationship (see Hos. 2:14-15,19). Even in her sin, God loved and cared for her. Although God might justly have abandoned the Hebrews because of their sinfulness, His divine compassion transcended divine justice (see Hos. 11:8-9).

17. Check the individuals for whom you have difficulty feeling compassion.

☐ **Homeless individuals** ☐ **Unwed mothers** ☐ **Addicts**
☐ **Obnoxious co-workers** ☐ **Prisoners** ☐ **Poor people**
☐ **A neighbor in grief** ☐ **Unsaved people** ☐ **Homosexuals**
☐ **Difficult family members**

Unlike us, God feels compassion toward people in spite of their sin. Isaiah compared God's concern for His people to a woman's labor pains (see Isa. 42:14). Like Hosea, Isaiah depicted God grieving over the Hebrews' unfaithfulness (see Isa. 63:10).

Several books in the Prophets describe God's withholding His wrath out of compassion for His people. Although His actions might seem inconsistent to us, we must recognize that God is not a vengeful tyrant but a compassionate, loving God who wants good for His children. Therefore, His compassion often led Him to exercise grace and mercy with an undeserving people. God alone is able to perfectly balance His justice with His mercy.

18. Read Jeremiah 18:7-10 and Jonah 3:10 in the margin. For what reason might God turn from His wrath?

_____

" 'At one moment I [God] might announce concerning a nation or a kingdom that I will uproot, tear down, and destroy it. However, if that nation I have made an announcement about, turns from its evil, I will not bring the disaster on it I had planned. At another time I announce that I will build and plant a nation or a kingdom. However, if it does what is evil in My sight by not listening to My voice, I will not bring the good I had said I would do to it.'"
Jeremiah 18:7-10

When people turn from their sin, God has compassion and receives them as His own. This divine compassion does not refer to a weakness in God's character but rather to His redemptive concern for us, His creation.

One of the worst aspects of suffering is a feeling of isolation. The Bible reminds us that God is with us in our suffering. Isaiah's prophecy of a child named Immanuel (God with us) provides a bridge between the Old Testament view of God as caring and

"God saw their actions—that they had turned from their evil ways—so God relented from the disaster He had threatened to do to them. And He did not do it."
Jonah 3:10

empathetic and the arrival of Jesus (see Isa. 7:14; Matt. 2:23). The same compassionate God who helped the Hebrews in the exodus and the exile also showed His compassion for humanity by coming to earth in the form of Jesus.

19. How does knowing Jesus help you feel God's compassion when you hurt?

Check your understanding of suffering in the Prophets by matching the themes with the books where they are found.

____ 1. Judges	a. Innocent suffering
____ 2. Amos and others	b. God's compassion
____ 3. Jeremiah and Ezekiel	c. Individual responsibility
____ 4. Isaiah	d. God's justice
____ 5. Daniel and others	e. Retribution
____ 6. Hosea	f. Redemptive suffering

Our survey of suffering in the Prophets has reinforced several themes found in the Pentateuch and has added some new ones. You should have answered 1. e, 2. a, 3. c, 4. f, 5. d, 6. b.

Suffering in the Writings

Writings
A miscellaneous collection of Bible books consisting of Poetic Books (Job, Psalms, Proverbs); the Festival Scrolls (Ruth, Esther Ecclesiastes, Song of Songs, Lamentations); and the Historical Books 1–2 Chronicles, Ezra, Nehemiah, Daniel)

The variety of responses to suffering in the Prophets shows the danger of using only one explanation of suffering to understand this complex issue. The Writings also challenge a simplistic, one-dimensional answer to suffering. As we study this division of the Old Testament, we will discover new treatments of familiar themes as well as some new ones. We will focus on five books in the Writings: Psalms, Proverbs, Job, Ecclesiastes, and Esther.

Psalms of Suffering

Written by several authors, the psalms reflect a wide variety of experiences across several centuries. Many passages praise God for His greatness and goodness, reminding worshipers of divine characteristics such as love or mercy or of a divine action such as creation. They affirm that although God is the Creator of the universe, He cares for His people. Frequently the Psalms refer to God's steadfast love, which is loyal despite the covenant partner's unfaithfulness. With confidence in God's goodness, several psalms refer to divine retribution, assuring readers that God will bring long-term consequences to both the righteous and the wicked (see Ps. 1). The largest category of Psalms, laments, emphasizes two additional themes.

Cries for justice. The writers of these Psalms cry out to God for deliverance from a problem such as sickness or abuse. Usually very candid about their concerns, the psalmists plead with God to act justly in their lives. In fact, they expect God to act on their behalf and promise to praise Him for His help. Some laments, such as Psalm 22, begin with a sense of abandonment: "My God, my God, why have You forsaken me?" (Ps. 22:1). But the writers find assurance that God will help, and they regain hope and confidence in God regardless of their difficult circumstances (see Ps. 22:22-24).

Some of the laments are so harsh that some people are cautious about using them in Christian public worship.[7] Called vengeance psalms, cursing psalms, or imprecatory psalms, these passages record desperate cries for divine justice. Sometimes the psalmist sounds vindictive as he calls on God to punish his enemies. In Psalm 109, for example, the psalmist urges God to kill his enemy and bring tragedy on the enemy's family (see vv. 6-20). To the Christian reader these psalms may be troublesome, but the psalmist was taking seriously traditional Hebrew beliefs: God's justice, retribution in this life, and the psalmist's identity with God's cause.[8]

We can appreciate the psalmists' total honesty and, more important, the fact that they turned to God in their distress. Apparently, the psalmists did not seek revenge but relied on God's justice, trusting that their struggles were in His hands.

"I will proclaim Your name to my brothers; I will praise You in the congregation. You who fear the LORD, praise Him! all you descendants of Jacob, honor Him! All you descendants of Israel, revere Him! For He has not despised or detested the torment of the afflicted. He did not hide His face from him, but listened when he cried to Him for help."
Psalm 22:22-24

20. How can we give our distress about injustices to God, demonstrating our willingness to let Him deal with it?
☐ Pray that God will punish our enemies and make them suffer.
☐ Pray that God will turn our enemies from their sinful ways.
☐ Pray that God will condone our vengeful attitude or actions

God will not condone our vengeance, because bringing judgment and justice is His role. The second prayer idea is most likely to align our wills with God's will for our enemies. However, God certainly understands when we ask Him to punish our enemies, as the psalmists often requested.

Questions about the doctrine of retribution. One experience that prompted the psalmists to question the doctrine of retribution was the prosperity of the wicked (see Pss. 37; 49; 73). Although the psalmists eventually expressed confidence in God's justice, these psalms reveal a deep reservation about the doctrine of retribution as a comprehensive explanation of suffering. The prosperity of the wicked seemed to refute the traditional idea that the wicked will suffer for their sin. It simply didn't make sense that good things happened to bad people. In the end the psalmists were usually assured that the prosperity of the wicked was only temporary. At some point in the future, justice would prevail (see Ps. 37:9-11,20-22). More importantly, the psalmists learned that God's continuing presence is more valuable than material rewards (see Ps. 73:23-25).

"I am always with You;
You hold my right hand.
You guide me with Your
counsel,
and afterwards You
will take me up
in glory.
Whom do I have
in heaven but You?
And I desire nothing
on earth but You."
Psalm 73:23-25

21. Give an example that frustrates you in each area today:

Apparent injustice: _____

The prosperity of the wicked: _____

The Psalms show us that when we feel oppressed by injustice, we can cry out to God while having full confidence that His divine justice will eventually prevail.

Wisdom in Suffering

The Hebrew wisdom books—Proverbs, Ecclesiastes, and Job—also address evil and suffering. Scholars often divide the Bible's wisdom writings into two broad categories:

- *Prudential wisdom* offers practical advice for living a successful life. The familiar discussion of the righteous and the wicked in Psalm 1, for example, reflects this approach. Proverbs also fits into this category.
- *Reflective wisdom* poses questions about the meaning of life and tends to be more critical or pessimistic than the prudential tradition. Psalm 73, for example, might be called a wisdom psalm in the reflective sense, along with Job and Ecclesiastes.

Let's first explore evil and suffering in the Book of Proverbs. In many ways Proverbs recalls our earlier discussions of the doctrine of retribution. For example, the writer often classified people in two categories: the wise and the foolish. These groups will be rewarded or punished according to their actions. Wise persons orient their lives to God (see Prov. 3:5-6). True wisdom is not mere human cleverness or skill but begins in the "fear of the LORD" (Prov. 1:7; 9:10). A fool is not someone with a low IQ but a person who does not respect God and rejects sound advice. This division of people into the wise and the foolish is similar to the two-ways-of-life concept in Deuteronomy and in many of the Prophets.

We can make three generalizations about the way the doctrine of retribution is treated in Proverbs.

> *"Trust in the LORD*
> *with all your heart,*
> *and do not rely on your*
> *own understanding;*
> *think about Him*
> *in all your ways,*
> *and He will guide you*
> *on the right paths."*
> Proverbs 3:5-6

Proverbs describes rewards and punishments as primarily material. Consistent with the view in the Pentateuch, Proverbs teaches that if people are good, they will normally receive long life (see Prov. 3:2), riches (see Prov. 3:16), honor (see Prov. 3:16), favor with God (see Prov. 12:2), health (see Prov. 3:8), relief from trouble (see Prov. 11:8), and many more benefits. Most consequences of actions named in Proverbs are available in this life.

22. Check the statements that reflect the teaching in Proverbs.
☐ **a. Being good always brings rewards in this life.**
☐ **b. We can cultivate prosperity by doing good.**
☐ **c. In general, righteousness brings rewards in this life.**

The writer of Proverbs was not encouraging a mercenary religion in which people are good in order to be rewarded. Instead, he simply stressed that a wise person will enjoy rewards. His teaching was a reflection of personal experience, not a foolproof promise that piety always pays. You should have checked statement *c*.

Proverbs stresses that retribution applies to individuals. While Deuteronomy and some of the Prophets stress collective retribution for the nation, tribe, or family, Proverbs generally emphasizes individual accountability. For example, several times in Proverbs an older person tells a young man to avoid loose women and to remain faithful to his spouse (see Prov. 5:1-6,15-23). Some proverbs

*"Idle hands make
one poor,
but diligent hands
bring riches.
The son who gathers
during summer
is prudent;
the son who sleeps
during harvest
is disgraceful."*
Proverbs 10:4-5

encourage workers to be industrious (see Prov. 6:6; 10:4-5). Gossip and lying bring harmful results (see Prov. 15:1-4; 17:9; 18:21).

Proverbs suggests that rewards and punishments are often built-in consequences of actions. Although some parts of the Old Testament stress God's direct involvement in dispensing rewards and punishments, Proverbs frequently describes consequences as the natural results of actions.[9]

23. If actions have built-in consequences, what can we conclude about our universe? Check all that apply.
☐ **a. God has built His sense of justice into the order of things.**
☐ **b. Absolute right and wrong do not exist.**
☐ **c. We live in a moral universe.**

The writer was confident that we live in a moral universe created by a just God *(a)*. His confidence in the moral order of things *(c)* allowed him to discuss the relationship between deeds and consequences without always mentioning God's involvement.

Learning Through Suffering

The Book of Job, another Wisdom book, describes one of the most detailed and graphic experiences of suffering anywhere. Job was a good, wealthy man who served God and cared for his family. Satan, however, challenged God to test Job's sincerity: "'Does Job fear God for nothing?'" (Job 1:9). Perhaps Job served God so faithfully because it paid off, Satan insisted. God allowed Satan to bring tragedy on Job and his family. While the prose prologue (Job 1–2) and epilogue (Job 42:7-17) present Job as a patient sufferer who refuses to reject God and is finally vindicated, the poetic heart of the book (Job 3:1–42:6) describes Job as perplexed about his suffering.

*"Consider: who has
perished when
he was innocent?
Where have the honest
been destroyed?
In my experience,
those who plow
injustice
and those who sow
trouble reap
the same."*
Job 4:7-8

Job's discussions with Eliphaz, Bildad, Zophar, and later Elihu point to the author's deep reservations about the doctrine of retribution as an explanation for Job's suffering. Job's friends came to "offer sympathy and comfort to him" (Job 2:11), but they eventually accused Job of harboring sin. In general, Job's friends supported a strict application of the principle of retribution and neglected to consider other explanations for his trials. Read in the margin Eliphaz's question when Job began to complain about his suffering.

24. On what did Eliphaz base his view of Job's circumstances?
☐ Job's life   ☐ A direct word from God   ☐ His own experience

What can be dangerous about attempting to analyze the reasons for another person's suffering? Check all that apply.
☐ We might be mistaken.
☐ We might help too much when God is trying to discipline.
☐ We might become judgmental.

We can encounter any of these problems when we try to analyze the reasons for another person's suffering.

As Job's friends defended the retributive principle, they made at least two mistakes.

- Job's comforters assumed that retribution is a reversible formula. Earlier I diagrammed retribution this way:

Bad ➡ suffering   Good ➡ success

As we saw in our discussion of Proverbs, this view is adequate as a general rule-of-thumb explanation for suffering. Normally, a good person will be better off in life than a bad person. Unfortunately, Job's friends attempted to reverse the formula:

Suffering ➡ bad   Success ➡ good

Because Job was suffering, the friends assumed he harbored terrible, unconfessed sin. As long as Job had prospered, they had assumed he was good. Now they assumed he was not.

- Job's friends insisted that the principle of retribution is the cause of all suffering. Taking a good rule-of-thumb explanation of suffering and universalizing it, these men believed that all sufferers are sinners. When we see people suffering, we need to avoid concluding that they must be suffering because of their sins. All people are sinners, but Job's suffering was not directly the result of his sin. In fact, at the end of the book God criticized Job's friends for not speaking the truth about Him (Job 42:7). Job's friends did not want to allow any exceptions to their theological system. They were really defending their theology rather than counseling Job.

> When we see people suffering, we need to avoid concluding that they must be suffering because of their sins.

*"Man born of woman
    is short of days
    and full of trouble."*
Job 14:1

*"Would you really
    challenge My justice?
Would you declare
    Me guilty to justify
    yourself?"*
Job 40:8

Job realized that some troubles are part of life (see Job 14:1), but he did not understand why he received so much suffering. Only the distribution, not the existence, of suffering perplexed him. Job appealed for an audience with God. Sometimes Job felt that God was his enemy (see Job 13:24-28; 16:9-14; 19:5-12,22), but he still wanted to meet with Him.[10] Although Job did not directly blame God for his suffering, he knew that God was sovereign and could provide answers. Job recognized that God was in charge of his life and was ultimately responsible for his suffering.

25. Read God's words in Job 40:8. Why did God take issue with Job?

_____

God appeared to Job and, instead of offering Job a simple explanation of suffering, emphasized His sovereignty over the universe. In confronting God, Job had crossed the line and questioned God's sense of justice. Although God never gave Job a reason for his suffering, Job grew in his knowledge of himself and God.

At the end of the book, Job responded to God:

*I had heard rumors about You,
but now my eyes have seen You.
Therefore I take back my words
and repent in dust and ashes.* Job 42:5-6

**26. What was Job repenting of? ☐ An arrogant attitude
☐ Unacknowledged sin ☐ Asking questions of God**

Job was not repenting for unacknowledged sin. He simply realized that he had disappointed God with his attitude. Job was not wrong to ask questions about his suffering, but at times he seemed to question God's justice and to impatiently demand that God appear on Job's timetable. God does not discourage us from asking questions about our hurts and troubles, but the Book of Job reminds us that there will always be an element of mystery to suffering. We should not expect a simplistic answer to a very complex problem. God's purpose in our suffering is beyond our knowledge and beyond our need to know.

The Book of Job helps us understand suffering in these ways.

- The doctrine of retribution cannot be used to explain the existence of all suffering.
- Although Satan is prominent in the opening chapters, Job never doubted that God is ultimately responsible for what happens. The Hebrews always avoided blaming suffering on Satan. God allowed Satan to test Job's faith (see Job 1:12; 2:6).
- We cannot fully understand why we suffer, but we can trust in God's sovereignty.
- Job matured through his suffering, teaching us that we can grow through our pain (see Job 5:17; 36:9-15).

27. What is the most valuable lesson you learned from Job?

_____

Questions from Suffering

Many find Ecclesiastes perplexing. Like Job, Ecclesiastes fits within the reflective-wisdom tradition, but its understanding of suffering is deeply disturbing to many of us. The book seems skeptical and pessimistic when compared to the optimism of Proverbs, and it seems to provide more questions than answers.

The author of Ecclesiastes, referred to as the Teacher in Ecclesiastes 1:1, had observed considerable injustice around him.

28. Read Ecclesiastes 4:1 in the margin. What did the Teacher observe about the oppressed?

_____

Read Ecclesiastes 7:15; 8:14 in the margin. What did the Teacher's experience tell him about the doctrine of retribution?

_____

The Teacher saw people being oppressed who had "no one to comfort them" (Eccl. 4:1). Through his experiences he had learned that the doctrine of retribution is not always a reliable rule, and he was troubled by the prosperity of the wicked (see Eccl. 7:15; 8:14).

"I observed all the acts of oppression being done under the sun. Look at the tears of those who are oppressed; they have no one to comfort them. Power is with those who oppress them; they have no one to comfort them."
Ecclesiastes 4:1

"In my futile life I have seen everything: there is a righteous man who perishes in spite of his righeousness, and there is a wicked man who lives long in spite of his evil."
Ecclesiastes 7:15

"There is a futility that is done on the earth: there are righeous people who get what the actions of the wicked deserve, and there are wicked people who get what the actions of the righeous deserve."
Ecclesiastes 8:14

The Teacher's major thesis seems to be "Absolute futility. Everything is futile" (Eccl. 1:2). But although the Teacher could not really understand God's ways in the world, he did not deny God.

29. Read Ecclesiastes 12:13-14 in the margin. What was the Teacher's advice for finding meaning in life?

"When all has been heard, the conclusion of the matter is: fear God and keep His commands, because this is for all humanity. For God will bring every act to judgment, including every hidden thing, whether good or evil."
Ecclesiastes 12:13-14

The Teacher advised finding meaning in life by seeking God. God alone brings meaning. A life lived apart from God ultimately brings futility and emptiness because secular pursuits do not satisfy.

What can we learn from Ecclesiastes about suffering? Like Job, the Teacher reminds us that we can be honest with God about our doubts and anxieties. After years of craving earthly pursuits, he reached a simple but profound conclusion: fear God and obey Him. An obedient relationship with God makes life worthwhile.

God's Providence

The story of Esther recounts how a young Jewish girl responded to evil and helped save her people from a massacre. It is set in the Persian period of Hebrew history, the period of reconstruction after the exile. Esther and her elderly cousin, Mordecai, lived in Persia during the reign of King Ahasuerus. When the king became displeased with Queen Vashti, he replaced her with Esther. Meanwhile, Mordecai saved the king from an assassination plot. Haman, a high Persian official, disliked Mordecai and conspired to have him and all Jews killed. Not realizing that Esther was Jewish, the king signed a decree authorizing the slaughter of the Jews. Mordecai sent a message to Esther alerting her to her strategic relationship to the king and her opportunity to save her people: "'Who knows, perhaps you have come to the kingdom for such a time as this'" (Esth. 4:14). Esther courageously approached the king and gained permission for her people to defend themselves. Eventually, Haman was hanged in the same gallows he had prepared for Mordecai's execution. The Jews escaped disaster and made the date of their deliverance a new holy day, Purim.

What does Esther's experience teach us about evil and suffering? It reminds us of God's providence and the role of key individuals in it. Mordecai urged Esther to become active in saving the Jewish people, though God could have chosen another way of deliverance. Even though God's name never appears in the book, the author obviously saw God's hand throughout the events. The account also supports the doctrine of retribution. For a while it seemed that Haman would be successful, but in the end he was executed.

The Book of Esther identifies a danger in our response to suffering. The story might tempt us to retaliate in the face of unjust treatment. The Jews defended themselves from slaughter, but they could have been tempted to go on the offensive (see Esth. 9:5). Self-defense may be a valid response to attack, but when self-defense is mixed with self-righteousness, the result can be a crusading attitude. When Christians mobilize to address a social problem, we should be careful to avoid simplistic solutions, and we should be careful not to use ungodly means to achieve our goals. The Jews' actions in the Book of Esther should not be used to support misguided attempts to correct the world's problems.

"The Jews put all their enemies to the sword, killing and destroying them. They did what they pleased to those who hated them."
Esther 9:5

30. Check appropriate ways for believers to respond to social problems.
☐ **a. Repay violence with violence.**
☐ **b. Take the law into our hands.**
☐ **c. Call and write lawmakers.**
☐ **d. Pray for and minister to individuals who suffer.**
☐ **e. Inform others of the problem or related issues.**

When suffering comes our way, we typically take flight or fight. When we flee from the human cause of our suffering, we miss an opportunity to see what God wants to accomplish through our suffering. If we misunderstand suffering, we may neglect to reach out to those who are hurting and could be restored. Some Hebrews, like the prophet Jonah, saw no need to reach out to the Gentiles. We should learn an important lesson from Esther: sometimes we must take a stand for right or for the oppressed even at high risk or great cost. God may have brought us to the opportunity " 'for such a time as this' " (Esth. 4:14). Statements *c, d,* and *e* are appropriate ways believers can respond to suffering in society.

Fear No Evil

Lessons from the Writings

In our survey of this division of the Old Testament, we have seen several perspectives on evil and suffering. The Book of Proverbs affirms that the doctrine of retribution explains a lot of our suffering: we generally get what we deserve in this life. However, the Writings place limitations on the retributive principle. In the Book of Job, Job's friends overemphasized the doctrine of retribution; they were reluctant to grant that Job's suffering was undeserved. Job himself, who suffered innocently, learned that some suffering is a mystery but that God's sovereignty can be trusted. Some of the psalms wrestle with the injustice of a world where the wicked prosper while good people suffer. The story of Esther reaffirms divine providence. Working behind the scenes, God enabled Esther to save her people from destruction.

The teachings in the Prophets and the Writings are not the final word on suffering. As we turn to the New Testament, we will see a variety of purposes for and responses to suffering. Most significantly, we will see Jesus, the Suffering Servant, who came to teach truth, compassion, and long-suffering for the cause of the gospel.

> **Some suffering is a mystery, but God's sovereignty can be trusted.**

---

[1] For a good selection of reactions, see Donald B. Kraybill and Linda Gehman Peachey, eds., *Where Was God on Sept. 11?* (Scottdale, PA: Herald Press, 2002).

[2] Arthur S. Peake, *The Problem of Suffering in the Old Testament* (London: Robert Bryant and C. H. Kelly, 1904), 1, 17.

[3] Edmund F. Sutcliffe, *Providence and Suffering in the Old and New Testaments* (London: Thomas Nelson and Sons, 1953), 108.

[4] John Paterson, *The Book That Is Alive: Studies in Old Testament Life and Thought as Set Forth by the Hebrew Sages* (New York: Charles Scribner's Sons, 1954), 90–91.

[5] Peake, *The Problem of Suffering*, 118–25; Harry Emerson Fosdick, *A Guide to Understanding the Bible: The Development of Ideas Within the Old and New Testaments* (New York: Harper and Brothers, 1938), 167–70; Daniel J. Simundson, *Faith Under Fire: Biblical Interpretations of Suffering* (Minneapolis: Augsburg, 1980), 111–22.

[6] Erhard S. Gerstenberger and Wolfgang Schrage, *Suffering*, trans. John E. Steely (Nashville: Abingdon, 1977), 98–102.

[7] Bernhard W. Anderson, *Out of the Depths: The Psalms Speak for Us Today*, rev. and expanded (Philadelphia: Westminster, 1983), 84.

[8] C. S. Lewis, *Reflections on the Psalms* (New York: Harcourt Brace Jovanovich, 1958), 9–33.

[9] W. Sibley Towner, *How God Deals with Evil* (Philadelphia: Westminster, 1976), 47–52.

[10] James L. Crenshaw, *A Whirlpool of Torment: Israelite Traditions of God as an Oppressive Presence* (Philadelphia: Fortress, 1984), 62–75.

Chapter 4

Jesus Reached Out with Compassion
Suffering in the Gospels and Acts

MILLIONS SAW MEL GIBSON'S POWERFUL MOVIE *The Passion of the Christ.* The film's graphic portrayal of Jesus' physical suffering shocked many long familiar with the Gospel accounts of Christ's death. *The Passion* certainly made one lesson clear: Jesus understood suffering. Not only did He address human hurt through His teachings and miracles, but He also endured suffering at its worst by dying an agonizing death on a Roman cross.

Because Jesus is the fullest revelation of God, our study of the New Testament perspective on evil and suffering starts with Him. In this chapter we will focus on Jesus' ministry to the hurting, as recorded in the Gospels, and its impact on the early Christians, as recorded in the Book of Acts. We will see that Jesus' life and early Christian history were punctuated with suffering and persecution; yet Jesus' life was also characterized by joy. Jesus brought a fresh perspective to the questions of why people suffer and what can be done to alleviate their hurt.

Jesus Came to Help Those Who Suffer

Yoke
A wooden bar that joined two draft animals, enabling them to work together

If you were not a Christian and turned to the New Testament for help with your problems, you might be perplexed. On one hand, you could find numerous passages that promise relief from struggles. For example, Jesus said, "'Come to Me, all of you who are weary and burdened, and I will give you rest'" (Matt. 11:28). On the other hand, these reassuring words are immediately followed by a text that stresses the acceptance of servitude: "'Take up My yoke and learn from Me'" (Matt. 11:29). "A yoke?" you might exclaim. "I want release from my suffering, not more suffering!"

This paradoxical passage is crucial to understanding Jesus' relationship to our suffering. He helps with our problems; yet being His disciple may bring different dilemmas. In spite of this risk, Jesus encourages us to come to Him: "'I am gentle and humble in heart, and you will find rest for yourselves. For My yoke is easy and My burden is light'" (Matt. 11:29-30). Indeed, Jesus' followers found relief for their problems through Him, and they learned that His abundant life outweighed any difficulty they faced for His sake. Jesus' yoke offered help and hope for the suffering in four ways.

Legalism
Imposing human rules for religious life that are unbiblical and burdensome or are based on the letter of the law without its spirit

Jesus offered relief from legalism. Many Jews were oppressed by the legalism of the Jewish religion.[1] Originally, the Hebrews had accepted God's law in gratitude for their liberation from Egypt. They could even celebrate the guidance the law gave them for daily living (see Ps. 119). Over the centuries, however, some religious leaders had interpreted the law to the point that it became burdensome and even impossible for the ordinary person to obey. Jesus frequently criticized these first-century leaders for oppressing the people through the law: "'Woe also to you experts in the law! You load people with burdens that are hard to carry'" (Luke 11:46).

1. What examples of legalism do you observe today?
☐ **Rigid requirements for church members' appearance**
☐ **Cultic practices of severe self-deprivation**
☐ **Dogmatic, unbiblical control by church members or leaders**
☐ **Insistence on a particular style of worship**
☐ **Other:** _____

Why is legalism so harmful? _____

Although Jesus did not intend to abolish the law, He came to relieve people of the burden of legalism (see Matt. 5:17-20), which distorts the true intent of God's law and judges others by human standards instead of God's. Jesus' priority was to serve people, not to enforce legalistic restrictions. Still, He had great expectations for His followers. The difference was that His yoke was easy and His burden was light when compared to Jewish legalism. The Greek word for *easy* means *well-fitting*. Yokes in the first century were tailor-made to fit each ox so that it would not be harmed. Similarly, Jesus' call on our lives is tailor-made to protect us from the suffering sin can bring.

Jesus offered God's love. Jesus pointed His followers to an understanding of God that would encourage rather than threaten them. God was not out to destroy them. He loved them and wanted them to be His children. Although He frequently spoke of divine judgment, He often reminded His audience of God's love and concern. For example, in the Sermon on the Mount Jesus pointed to the futility of anxiety in light of God's care (see Matt. 6:25-34).

2. Read the following verses in the margins on pages 77–78. Match the Scripture references with the ways God cares for us.

____ 1. Matthew 6:31-32 a. God will help us know what to say and do when persecuted.

____ 2. Matthew 7:11

____ 3. Luke 12:6-7 b. We can give Him our cares.

____ 4. Luke 12:11-12 c. He wants to give us good gifts.

____ 5. 1 Peter 5:6-7 d. We are too valuable for Him to forget us.

 e. He knows and provides for our needs.

I hope you matched the verses this way: 1. e, 2. c, 3. d, 4. a, 5. b.

Jesus offered accessibility to God. In His parables Jesus highlighted God's accessibility, assuring people of God's interest in their needs and His faithfulness to provide for those who ask Him. Jesus told of a man who got out of bed late at night to provide bread for a neighbor who had unexpected company (see Luke 11:5-8). Explaining the story to His disciples, Jesus focused on God's willingness to respond to our requests: "'Keep asking, and it will be given to you. Keep searching, and you will find. Keep knocking,

"'Don't worry, saying, "What will we eat?" or "What will we drink?" or "What will we wear?" For the idolaters eagerly seek all these things, and your heavenly Father knows you need them.'"
Matthew 6:31-32

"'If you then, who are evil, know how to give good gifts to your children, how much more will your Father in heaven give good things to those who ask Him!'"
Matthew 7:11

"'Aren't five sparrows sold for two pennies? Yet not one of them is forgotten in God's sight. Indeed, the hairs of your head are all counted. Don't be afraid; you are worth more than many sparrows.'"
Luke 12:6-7

*"'Whenever they bring
you before synagogues
and rulers and authori-
ties, don't worry about
how you should defend
yourselves or what you
should say. For the
Holy Spirit will teach
you at that very hour
what must be said.'"*
Luke 12:11-12

*"Humble yourselves
therefore under the
might hand of God,
so that He may
exalt you in due time,
casting all your care
upon Him, because
He cares about you."*
1 Peter 5:6-7

*"'May they all be one,
as You, Father, are in
Me and I am in You.
May they also be one
in Us, so the world may
believe You sent Me.'"*
John 17:21

and the door will be opened to you'" (Luke 11:9). Later, Jesus told a similar parable about a persistent widow who finally wore down a cantankerous judge. Jesus noted that God willingly responds to our requests, not begrudgingly like the unjust judge (see Luke 18:1-8). God wants to help those who come to Him in need and pain.

3. Read John 17:21 in the margin. How does a believer's relationship with God give us access to Him?
☐ **All people have open access to God at any time.**
☐ **We are inseparably linked with God through Christ.**
☐ **God connects with believers when He is ready to do so.**

Our relationship with God gives us access to Him because we are inseparably linked with Him through Christ. This access means that God is available to help when we suffer and that we can share with others the good news that God cares when they hurt.

Jesus offered a relationship with God. Jesus taught that by becoming followers of Christ, individuals are literally adopted into God's family. Occasionally, Jesus used the term *Abba* for God. The Aramaic word *Abba*, which meant *papa* or *daddy*, refers to God as Father in a personal, intimate way. Jesus' use of this term indicated to others that God is truly a compassionate Father (see Mark 14:36). Later Paul explained that we Christians also have the privilege of addressing God as *Abba* (see Rom. 8:15).

4. How do you view God? Check any that apply.
☐ **As a loving, protective Father**
☐ **As a harsh, punitive Father**
☐ **As a distant, unattached Father**

God wants to relate to us as a loving, protective Father who provides for our needs. If you marked one or both of the last two responses, consider talking with your group-study leader or pastor about developing a close relationship with a loving God who will become a gentle Father to you. When we are in a right relationship with God through Jesus Christ, we can have confidence that He cares for us in our suffering as a Father cares for a child.

Following Christ Can Bring Suffering

Although Jesus came to offer release from various burdens, we must also recognize that being His disciple can bring suffering. Dietrich Bonhoeffer's life and death illustrate the reality of suffering for Christ. Bonhoeffer was a critic of Hitler and the Nazi movement in Germany in the 1930s and 1940s. He was eventually arrested and hanged. Several years before, Bonhoeffer wrote, "When Christ calls a man, he bids him come and die."[2]

5. Read Luke 9:23 in the margin and then explain what you think Bonhoeffer's words mean.

_____

"'If anyone wants to come with Me, he must deny himself, take up his cross daily, and follow Me.'"
Luke 9:23

Even though every Christian is not martyred as Bonhoeffer was, we are all called to deny our old way of life, live by the Spirit of Christ, and embrace the mission God has for us to do.

Jesus taught His followers that they would face opposition for following Him: "'If they persecuted Me, they will also persecute you'" (John 15:20). Many people were undoubtedly impressed with Jesus' authority in teaching and performing miracles, but His emphasis on the price of discipleship may have deterred some.

Being a disciple in the first century eventually meant opposition from both the Jews and the Romans. The opening chapters of Acts describe the high cost of being a believer, as well as Christians' courage in the face of adversity. The rapid growth of the church in Jerusalem no doubt contributed to its visibility and eventual persecution. Arrested and imprisoned, the Christian leaders were ordered to stop preaching, but they felt a compulsion to continue telling the world about Jesus, no matter what the consequences (see Acts 4:13-21). "'We must obey God rather than men'" (Acts 5:29), they insisted. Instead of trying to avoid persecution, the people rejoiced "that they were counted worthy to be dishonored on behalf of the name" (Acts 5:41).

Stephen became the first Christian martyr when an enraged Sanhedrin executed him (see Acts 7). The great persecution that followed his death forced Christians to leave Jerusalem (see Acts 8:1-3; 11:19). Many other believers suffered persecution at Paul's hands before his conversion, and Herod Agrippa I also attacked the Jerusalem church (see Acts 12). During the reign of Emperor Claudius (see Acts 18:1-2), Jews and Christians clashed over Jesus in Rome about A.D. 49. The cost of following Christ was high.

Jesus never commanded His disciples to seek suffering. Rather, He realistically alerted His followers to the type of resistance they could expect by following Him. We should not try to measure our devotion by how much we suffer. We are not called to be masochists, seeking pain, but followers of Jesus live with the reality that we may suffer because of our loyalty to Christ.

6. In what ways have you encountered opposition for following Christ? Check all that apply.
☐ **Misunderstanding**   ☐ **Ridicule**   ☐ **Trouble at work**
☐ **Strained relationships** ☐ **Rejection**   ☐ **Pain**
☐ **Loss of possessions** ☐ **Imprisonment** ☐ **No opposition**

Was the sacrifice worth it?   ☐ **Yes**   ☐ **No**
Did this opposition cause you to stop proclaiming Christ?
☐ **Yes**   ☐ **No**

"As He stepped ashore, He saw a huge crowd, felt compassion for them, and healed their sick."
Matthew 14:14

"Moved with compassion, Jesus touched their eyes. Immediately they could see, and they followed Him."
Matthew 20:34

"Moved with compassion, Jesus reached out His hand and touched him. 'I am willing,' He told him. 'Be made clean.'"
Mark 1:41-42

Jesus Showed Compassion for the Suffering

Jesus devoted His life to ministry that relieved suffering. Peter later summarized Jesus' public ministry by stressing "how He went about doing good" (Acts 10:38). Jesus frequently responded to suffering people by performing miracles that relieved their pain.

7. Read the passages in the margin. What was Jesus' motivation for helping these people?

In these poignant cases of suffering, Jesus was moved by compassion to relieve suffering. But even our basic physical and spiritual needs stir His concern and care for us. Faced with a crowd of four thousand hungry people, Jesus responded, "'I have compassion on the crowd'" (Mark 8:2). The Greek word for *compassion* means *to radically identify with the needs of another person*. Jesus' followers knew, of course, that God had identified Himself as compassionate (see Ex. 22:27) and that several Hebrew writers had described Him that way (see Ex. 34:6-7; Lam. 3:32). However, Jesus' miracles provided living illustrations of the empathy that characterizes God the Father. The miracles gave people a deeper understanding of the way God relates to human need. Jesus did not perform miracles merely to attract attention to Himself. Rather, motivated by compassion, He worked wonders designed to help those who suffered.

Jesus' miracles can be classified into four types.

Exercising authority over nature. In performing nature miracles, Jesus controlled the forces of the physical world. For example, when He calmed the stormy sea (see Mark 4:35-41) or walked on the water (see Matt. 14:22-27), Jesus displayed His power over natural forces that may threaten our lives. He proved that He has authority over nature. His miracles of feeding the five thousand and the four thousand revealed Jesus' concern to help the hungry (see Mark 6:39-44; 8:6-9). He took the lesson a step farther by offering the large crowds Himself as the Bread of life (see John 6:35). Jesus satisfies both physical and spiritual hunger.

8. If possible, identify a time when you knew that God miraculously provided for your needs or protected you in the midst of storms—natural, personal, emotional, or spiritual.

Healing. As Jesus healed the blind, lame, leprous, and many others, He demonstrated His power over sickness and physical disability. He reminded observers that the power of healing is ultimately God's, through whom all things are possible (see Mark 10:27). Yet Jesus also involved people in their healing by pointing out the importance of human faith (see Mark 5:34).

9. Read Mark 5:34 in the margin. Why do you think Jesus introduced the subject of faith?

" 'Daughter,' He said to her, 'your faith has made you well. Go in peace and be free from your affliction.' "
Mark 5:34

Jesus did not divide the physical and the spiritual dimensions of human nature into separate compartments. He ministered to the total person, and He offered more than mere physical health. He cared about every need the person had.

10. Do you believe that God heals people today? ☐ Yes ☐ No
Does God always heal people physically?   ☐ Yes ☐ No
Why do you think God would choose not to heal physically?

_____

We may not understand why God doesn't always bring physical healing in this life. Jesus' examples of healing show that whether or not He healed physically, His goal for the person was spiritual wholeness and abundant life through a relationship with Himself.

Exorcising demons. Jesus' exorcisms demonstrated His authority over the forces of nature and the human body. Some of Jesus' most dramatic miracles involved casting out demons. Frequently, Jesus encountered people who were controlled by supernatural forces that prompted strange behavior. By restoring those people to normal human existence (see Mark 5:13-15), Jesus defeated the forces of evil and demonstrated His authority over the spiritual world.

11. Read the verses in the margin and complete the statements.
a. John 17:15: We are not removed from the troubles of the
   world, but we are _____ against
   any spiritual damage from Satan.
b. 2 Thessalonians 3:3: When we encounter evil, God will
   _____ and _____
   us, keeping us from Satan's death grip.
c. 2 Timothy 4:18: Satan's work will not affect my _____
   passage into God's heavenly kingdom even though I may
   encounter his efforts on earth.
d. 1 John 5:18: When Jesus is holding on to our hearts, the evil
   one can't even _____ us.

Reviving the dead. On three occasions Jesus raised the dead (see Mark 5:21-43; Luke 7:11-17; John 11:1-46). In each case Jesus' intervention graciously extended the length of life on earth. It also foreshadowed the eternal life He would provide to those who trust

" 'I [Jesus] am not praying that You [God] take them out of the world but that You protect them from the evil one [Satan].' "
John 17:15

"The Lord is faithful; He will strengthen and guard you from the evil one."
2 Thessalonians 3:3

"The Lord will rescue me from every evil work and will bring me safely into His heavenly kingdom."
2 Timothy 4:18

"We know that everyone who has been born of God does not sin, but the One [Jesus] who is born of God keeps him, and the evil one does not touch him."
1 John 5:18

and obey Him. Incorporating His power over the natural, physical, and spiritual worlds, these wonders proved that Jesus works under God's authority. Command over life and death belongs to Him.

Jesus touched people where they suffered physically, emotionally, and spiritually. Soon after He began His public ministry, He went to His hometown, Nazareth, to worship in the synagogue. There He read a passage from Isaiah that defined His ministry.

12. Read Luke 4:18-19 in the margin. Identify ways people today can be poor, captive, blind, and oppressed in each category.

	PHYSICALLY	EMOTIONALLY	SPIRITUALLY
Poor	_____	_____	_____
Captive	_____	_____	_____
Blind	_____	_____	_____
Oppressed	_____	_____	_____

"The Spirit of the Lord is on Me, because He has anointed Me to preach good news to the poor. He has sent Me to proclaim freedom to the captives and recovery of sight to the blind, to set free the oppressed, to proclaim the year of the Lord's favor."
Luke 4:18-19

Throughout His ministry Jesus reached out to those who were hurting, had compassion on them, and healed them. He always met them at the point of their need, sometimes by healing them physically or emotionally. But as the Great Physician, His ultimate concern was always their spiritual wholeness.

Jesus Taught His Disciples to Have Compassion for the Suffering

Jesus not only expressed His compassion for the suffering but also expected His disciples to have deep compassion and concern for the suffering. He said, "'Be compassionate as your Father is compassionate'" (Luke 6:36, NEB), and Jesus often encouraged a compassionate lifestyle. The parable of the good Samaritan, for example, highlighted the Samaritan's compassion, which prompted his humanitarianism (see Luke 10:33). Jesus' famous teaching on the judgment of the sheep and goats again pointed to the necessity of helping those who suffer (see Matt. 25:31-46). Jesus' disciples were to make feeding the hungry, giving a drink to the thirsty, welcoming the stranger, clothing the naked, and visiting the sick and imprisoned their priorities. Through these actions they would effectively share the good news of Jesus' compassion and love.

13. In which of these ministries are you currently involved?
☐ **Feeding the hungry** ☐ **Giving clothing to the needy**
☐ **Visiting prisoners** ☐ **Visiting the sick**
☐ **Visiting the homebound** ☐ **Sharing the gospel**
☐ **Offering shelter** ☐ **Other:** _____

The Book of Acts records several instances when the disciples followed Jesus' example of serving the suffering. Through God's power some disciples even healed the sick and raised the dead (see Acts 3:1-10; 9:36-41; 20:9-12; 28:8). The Jerusalem church also worked to alleviate poverty and hunger. By pooling their physical resources, the early Christians in Jerusalem eliminated poverty in their midst (see Acts 2:44-45; 4:32-35).

How much suffering could be eliminated today if committed Christians would sacrificially give to causes such as the alleviation of world hunger, poverty, and homelessness? In the small Oklahoma town where I live, several churches help provide shelter and food for the homeless. Each week a church opens its facilities to homeless people, and church members prepare meals and serve as hosts for those who need to spend the night. Christians are living the compassionate lifestyle Jesus demonstrated and encouraged.

"The multitude of those who believed were of one heart and soul, and no one said that any of his possessions was his own, but instead they held everything in common. And with great power the apostles were giving testimony to the resurrection of the Lord Jesus, and great grace was on all of them. For there was not a needy person among them, because all those who owned lands or houses sold them, brought the proceeds of the things that were sold, and laid them at the apostles' feet. This was then distributed to each person as anyone had a need."
Acts 4:32-35

14. How do a ministry and a humanitarian effort differ?
☐ **Church members engage in humanitarian efforts; church staff do ministry.**
☐ **A ministry is service in Jesus' name that addresses spiritual needs. Humanitarian efforts are merely good deeds done without mentioning Jesus.**
☐ **There is no distinguishable difference.**
Which would Jesus have us do?
☐ **Humanitarian efforts**   ☐ **Ministry**

Ministry is service in Jesus' name; humanitarian efforts take care of physical needs but may never mention Jesus. We must remember that while addressing physical hunger and thirst, Jesus also offered Himself as the Bread of life (see John 6:35,48) and the Living Water (see John 4:10). We must minister to people with compassion, not only by providing for their physical needs but also by sharing Christ as the answer to all of their needs—physical, mental, and spiritual.

15. Pray about becoming involved in a ministry.

Jesus Taught on Suffering

What did Jesus say about the origin of suffering? Only rarely did He address its root cause. In some passages Jesus attributed suffering to the doctrine of retribution, assuming that actions have consequences. In other passages He denied that the concept of retribution explained specific cases of suffering.

Suffering can be punishment for sin. When Jesus seemed to support the doctrine of retribution, He usually followed the Hebrew pattern of describing two choices—obedience and life, disobedience and death. For example, in the Sermon on the Mount Jesus compared these two ways of life with three word pictures: two gates, two trees, and two house builders (see Matt. 7:13-27). The comparison of the two housebuilders is perhaps the most graphic. One man built on a sandy foundation and the other on a solid rock foundation. When the rains and floods came, only the latter house could stand. Both men received the consequences of their choices.

In His parable of the rich man and Lazarus, Jesus illustrated the radically different consequences of being rich and callous toward the poor and being poor (see Luke 16:19-31). Abraham pointed out the reversal in fortunes after death: " 'Son, … remember that during your life you received your good things, just as Lazarus received bad things, but now he is comforted here, while you are in agony' " (Luke 16:25). In a parable about a great marriage feast, Jesus mentioned that inviting the poor and needy will bring a future reward (see Luke 14:14). Another time Jesus' disciples mentioned what they had given up to follow Him.

16. Read Luke 18:29-30 in the margin. When will Jesus' followers receive their reward?

_____

Jesus suggested that His followers would be rewarded in this life *and* in the age to come. In these passages and others, Jesus generally followed the traditional view that our actions earn eventual rewards and punishments.

" 'I assure you: There is no one who has left a house, wife or brothers, parents or children because of the kingdom of God, who will not receive many times more at this time, and eternal life in the age to come.' "
Luke 18:29-30

Although Jesus often spoke of rewards and punishments for sin, He did not always encourage us to apply the principle of retribution to others or ourselves. In the Sermon on the Mount, for example, Jesus discouraged seeking retaliation: "'You have heard that it was said, An eye for an eye and a tooth for a tooth. But I tell you, don't resist an evildoer'" (Matt. 5:38-39).

> "'If there is an injury, then you must give life for life, eye for eye, tooth for tooth, hand for hand, foot for foot, burn for burn, bruise for bruise, wound for wound.'"
> Exodus 21:23-25

17. Read Exodus 21:23-25 in the margin. How did Jesus' teaching differ from the Old Testament's teaching of "eye for eye"?

The "eye for eye, tooth for tooth" principle in the Old Testament, which we studied in chapter 2, had placed a limit on revenge, but Jesus wanted to completely remove our desire for personal retaliation. When James and John wanted to call down fire to destroy a Samaritan village that refused to welcome them, Jesus rebuked the disciples (see Luke 9:51-56). Although the village was not destroyed, it reaped an obvious consequence of its action: it missed the blessing of having Jesus visit, perhaps to perform miracles and teach. Jesus refused to punish the village, instead leaving it to the natural consequences of a poor choice.

Suffering is not always payment for sin. When Jesus encountered specific cases of suffering, He rarely linked them with sin. He most closely approached using retribution to explain suffering when He healed someone in conjunction with forgiving his or her sins. For example, when Jesus encountered a paralytic, He responded, "'Have courage, son, your sins are forgiven'" (Matt. 9:2).

18. Did Jesus mean the man's sin caused his illness? ☐ Yes ☐ No

Jesus did not explicitly say that the man's sins caused his paralysis, and it would be dangerous to use such a passage to claim Jesus' explicit support of retribution as an explanation of disease. On another occasion Jesus healed a paralyzed man on the sabbath. Meeting the man again, Jesus commented: "'See, you are well. Do not sin any more, so that something worse doesn't happen to you'" (John 5:14). Although some would argue that Jesus suggested that sin directly causes illness, He was probably merely cautioning the man not to let sin cause other suffering and problems in his life.

On two other occasions Jesus refused to link sin and suffering in a cause-effect relationship. When Jesus was told about the deaths of several Galileans at Pilate's hand, He asked: "'Do you think that these Galileans were more sinful than all Galileans because they suffered these things? No, I tell you; but unless you repent, you will all perish as well!'" (Luke 13:2-3). The Galileans did not die because they were more wicked than their countrymen.

Jesus then introduced another example of 18 people who were killed when the tower of Siloam fell on them.

19. Read Luke 13:4-5 in the margin and answer the questions.
Did Jesus explain why these were killed? ☐ **Yes** ☐ **No**
Did He imply their deaths resulted from sin? ☐ **Yes** ☐ **No**
Is His point more about sin than suffering? ☐ **Yes** ☐ **No**

"'Those 18 that the tower in Siloam fell on and killed—do you think they were more sinful than all the people who live in Jerusalem? No, I tell you; but unless you repent, you will all perish as well!'"
Luke 13:4-5

In these examples of moral suffering (killing by Pilate) and natural suffering (the tower falling), Jesus rejected a direct cause-effect relationship between these victims' sins and their deaths.

Our modern experiences with suffering confirm the validity of Jesus' refusal to link all sin and suffering. When tornadoes strike Oklahoma every spring, they usually cause widespread destruction. The tornadoes do not typically strike the homes of sinners and spare the homes of Christians. Therefore, we cannot jump to conclusions about the spiritual conditions of victims of natural disasters.

Jesus also addressed the doctrine of retribution when He met a blind man. His disciples asked, "'Rabbi, who sinned, this man or his parents, that he was born blind?'" (John 9:2). The disciples apparently held to a rigid form of the retributive principle, including the idea that punishment could be transferred across generations.

20. Read John 9:3 in the margin. How did Jesus respond to the disciples' question?
☐ **The man sinned.** ☐ **The man's parents sinned.**
☐ **Neither the man nor his parents sinned.**

"'Neither this man nor his parents sinned. ... This came about so that God's works might be displayed in him.'"
John 9:3

Jesus responded that retribution does not work this way. Sin did not cause the man's blindness, but because he was blind, Jesus could glorify God by healing him.[3] Jesus was devoted to ministering to suffering people rather than trying to explain why they suffered.

Suffering strikes everyone. In addition to rejecting the doctrine of retribution as a comprehensive explanation of human suffering, Jesus occasionally noted that suffering comes to all people—the good and the bad. He acknowledged God's indiscriminate treatment of humankind when He said that God " 'causes His sun to rise on the evil and the good, and sends rain on the righteous and the unrighteous' " (Matt. 5:45). If God operated by a strict retributive principle, the sun should shine only on the just, and rain should fall only on the unjust. When Lazarus died, his sisters, Mary and Martha, asked Jesus to come help: " 'Lord, the one You love is sick' " (John 11:3). They felt the Lord should extend special favor to those He loves. If their theory had been correct, we could expect that someone who followed Christ would be exempt from pain. But Christ's teaching never supported such a theory.

"Do not bring us into temptation, but deliver us from the evil one."
Matthew 6:13

21. Read Matthew 6:13 and John 16:33 in the margin.
Can we be protected from Satan? ☐ Yes ☐ No
Will we always be protected from problems? ☐ Yes ☐ No

How do you reconcile the fact that we can be protected from Satan's atacks while remaining vulnerable to hardship?

_____

" 'I have told you these things so that in Me you may have peace. You will have sufferings in this world. Be courageous! I have conquered the world.' "
John 16:33

Jesus encouraged us to pray for protection from Satan, but He did not promise that we would escape all suffering. Jesus raised Lazarus from the dead, but Jesus did not protect him from hurt because of His affection for him. Jesus compassionately responded to disease, but He did not intervene to alleviate all suffering.

22. Think of a believer you know who has suffered greatly.
How does Jesus' teaching explain this situation?
☐ This person suffers because of sin.
☐ Suffering comes to everyone, good and bad.
☐ This person lacks faith.

Jesus' response reminds us that we cannot blame all suffering on the doctrine of retribution. Hurt and pain are part of life in a fallen world. No one is exempt.

> Hurt and pain are part of life in a fallen world. No one is exempt.

23. Check your understanding of Jesus' teachings on suffering by marking each statement *T* (true) or *F* (false).

____ a. Jesus was more concerned about addressing the cure for suffering than about its cause.

____ b. Jesus taught that some suffering is caused by sin.

____ c. Jesus taught that we will be rewarded for helping those who suffer.

____ d. Jesus taught that we should be more concerned about immediate rewards than future rewards.

____ e. Jesus taught that we will be rewarded for following Him even if we suffer in this life.

____ f. Jesus explicitly taught that all suffering is caused by sin.

____ g. Jesus taught that He healed only to alleviate suffering.

____ h. Jesus taught that only the bad will experience suffering.

____ i. Jesus taught that it is more important to focus on spiritual needs than on physical needs.

Now check your answers: a. T, b. T, c. T, d. F, e. T, f. F, g. F, h. F, i. T.

The doctrine of retribution reappears in the Book of Acts. During the early years of the church, God punished several people for disobedience. Ananias and Sapphira both dropped dead after lying about the sale of their estate (see Acts 5:1-11). God killed Herod Agrippa I for allowing the people to worship him as divine (see Acts 12:21-23). Elymas the magician was struck blind when he tried to intervene in Paul's witnessing to Sergius Paulus (see Acts 13:11).

As we have seen, sin often leads to punishment. However, certain Old Testament Scriptures, along with some of Jesus' teachings, suggest that we must avoid universalizing the connection between sin and suffering.

Jesus Suffered

We will conclude our look at Jesus' relationship to suffering by considering the persecution and pain He endured on earth. The words "Jesus wept" (John 11:35) are interesting because they point to Jesus' genuine humanity. Jesus' first disciples probably had no difficulty affirming His humanity, for they saw Him angry, hungry, thirsty, and tired. But though Jesus frequently announced the coming suffering and death that would define His life's purpose (see Mark 9:30-32; 10:33-34), the disciples never seemed to fully understand or appreciate His words.

24. Why was it so difficult for the disciples to understand that Jesus would have to suffer? Check all that apply.
☐ **They thought the Messiah would come in power, not in submission to suffering.**
☐ **They had seen His miracles of healing and thought He would escape His own suffering.**
☐ **They didn't see any purpose for His suffering.**
☐ **They had forgotten the teachings in Scripture.**

"He was led like a sheep to the slaughter, and as a lamb is silent before its shearer, so He does not open His mouth. In His humiliation justice was denied Him. Who will describe His generation? For His life is taken from the earth."
Acts 8:32-33

Jesus' ministry modeled that of the Suffering Servant described in Isaiah, but the Jews did not expect the Messiah to suffer. To them a suffering Messiah was a contradiction in terms. They expected the Messiah to be a victorious military leader.

Only after the resurrection did Christians begin to fully understand the purpose of Jesus' suffering. When the risen Jesus walked with the two travelers to Emmaus, He explained again that He had to suffer: "'Didn't the Messiah have to suffer these things and enter into His glory?'" (Luke 24:26). In the early sermons, recorded in Acts, the disciples stressed that Jesus' death was essential to His ministry (see Acts 3:18). By the time Philip encountered the Ethiopian man, who was reading one of Isaiah's songs about the Servant, early Christians knew that Christ's suffering had been essential to accomplishing His purpose. Therefore, Philip pointed to Jesus as the fulfillment of Isaiah's message (see Acts 8:32-35).

"Christ also suffered for sins once for all, the righteous for the unrighteous, that He might bring you to God, after being put to death in the fleshly realm but made alive in the spiritual realm."
1 Peter 3:18

25. Read Acts 8:32-33 and 1 Peter 3:18 in the margin. How would you explain to an unbeliever why Jesus had to suffer and die?

_____

_____

_____

These verses show that Christ's suffering was innocent, redemptive, and vicarious. As Isaiah predicted, Jesus suffered and died on the cross to pay the penalty for our sin, thereby giving us His righteousness and making us right with God.

Jesus' suffering, crucifixion, and resurrection are essential to our Christian faith and especially to our understanding of suffering. Jesus suffered greatly during Passion Week. Although the week began with a large triumphal entry, the crowds soon rejected Him. Over the following days Jesus experienced the pain of being betrayed by one of the 12 apostles and being deserted by the others. He experienced the agony of daily interrogation and harassment in the temple. In the garden of Gethsemane, Jesus wrestled with God's will for His life. His agony in the garden was genuine (see Mark 14:33-42), but He willingly accepted the cross. Jesus endured the humiliation of being falsely accused; a series of mock trials or hearings; torture; and a slow, agonizing death on a cross. Perhaps Jesus' deepest suffering came when He felt abandoned by God: " 'My God, My God, why have You forsaken Me?' " (Mark 15:34).

What can we learn from Jesus' response to terrible suffering?

Passion
Jesus' extreme suffering

Passion Week
The week beginning with Palm Sunday and moving through Good Friday to Resurrection Sunday

Jesus did not retaliate against His accusers. When Jesus was attacked, He did not flee or fight. He warned His disciples against the use of force (see Matt. 26:52), and He forgave His executioners (see Luke 23:34). Certainly, His response was not expected by the Zealots, who used violence to attempt to overthrow the hated Roman government. Jesus practiced what He preached. " 'Love your enemies' " (Matt. 5:44) was more than a slogan to Him.

Zealots
The extreme, nationalistic wing of the Pharisees who, believing that only God had the right to rule over the Jews, advocated rebellion against the Roman Empire

26. What does Jesus' example teach us about our response to suffering for the sake of the gospel? Check all that apply.
☐ **We should not take the law into our hands.**
☐ **We must love and pray for our enemies.**
☐ **It's all right to use violence to achieve kingdom results.**
☐ **We should forgive those who persecute us.**

Jesus' example teaches us not to retaliate against those who persecute us when we take a stand for Christ. We should not use force or violence against them but should forgive them, love them, and pray for them.

Jesus' attitude toward His death represents Scripture's paradoxical view. Scripture depicts death as both an enemy to be avoided and the necessary means to a good purpose.

27. For Jesus, why was death both an enemy and something He embraced?

As a human, Jesus apparently did not want to die (see Mark 14:36), but He was willing to do so because it would carry out God's plan for the salvation of sinners. Jesus was an innocent victim, like the Servant of the Lord in Isaiah, dying on behalf of the guilty (see Isa. 53:5-6,10). Jesus was not suicidal, nor did He have a martyr complex, but He recognized that His suffering was essential to God's design for addressing the problem of sin.

The same is true of believers who have given their lives for Christ throughout history. Stephen was the first Christian martyr (see Acts 7:57-60). After his death great persecution was unleashed on the early church. Yet Acts 8:4 tells us that those who fled to escape persecution spread the good news to all parts of the world.

28. What good can come from the persecution and martyrdom of Christ's servants today? _____

Today believers around the world suffer and die for Christ. These tragedies, however, can bring eternal spiritual results by galvanizing the church and issuing a powerful testimony to the world that a commitment to Christ is worth dying for.

"I have been crucified with Christ; and I no longer live, but Christ lives in me. The life I now live in the flesh, I live by faith in the Son of God, who loved me and gave Himself for me."
Galatians 2:19-20

29. Read Galatians 2:19-20 in the margin. Why is death a good thing for a believer? _____

Dying to self is not only good but also necessary if Christ is to live His life in us.

Jesus' death was the ultimate revelation of God's identification with His people. The pain Jesus felt from the crowds' rejection reflects pain in God's heart. Throughout history God had grieved over His rejection by the Hebrews, much as a husband grieves over his wife's unfaithfulness. Jesus' death for human sin mirrors God's pain over our sin. As one scholar noted, "There was a cross in the heart of God before there was one planted on the green hill outside of Jerusalem. And now that the cross of wood has been taken down, the one in the heart of God abides, and it will remain so long as there is one sinful soul for whom to suffer."[4] Jesus' pain and the Father's pain are linked to the sinfulness of humankind.

Jesus' resurrection proclaims that Jesus came not only to minister to the suffering but also to overcome suffering. His death and resurrection defeated the supernatural forces that directly caused much evil. Then why didn't the resurrection end suffering? Jesus' life, ministry, death, and resurrection can be compared to D-Day in World War II, the decisive, turning-point battle in the war in Europe. Although fighting continued for a while longer, the ultimate outcome of the war was clear. The war did not stop, however, until V-Day. Jesus' death and resurrection represent the defeat of evil, but routing the forces of evil will continue until the end of time. Today we live in the tension between the *already* of Christ's resurrection and the *not yet* of the final elimination of suffering.

> **Routing the forces of evil will continue until the end of time.**

30. How does Christ's victory over sin and death help you as you observe or experience suffering? Check all that apply.
☐ **Helps me understand that suffering is only temporary**
☐ **Assures me that He understands suffering since He endured it**
☐ **Assures me that He will give comfort in suffering**
☐ **Helps me know that I too will be victorious as I trust Him**
☐ **Other:** _____

The Holy Spirit Is Our Comforter When We Suffer

In Jesus' farewell discourse He told the disciples that He would not leave them orphans (see John 14:18). In John 14:16 Jesus promised them the help of the Holy Spirit—the *paracletos*, a Greek word that is translated *Comforter* (KJV), *Advocate* (NEB), *Counselor* (HCSB, NIV), or *Helper* (GNT). This term refers to someone who is called alongside another person to help. Jesus described the Holy Spirit as our Helper in difficult situations. The older translation, *Comforter*, may be misleading today because we do not understand this word well. *Comfort* originally came from the Latin word *fortis*, meaning *bravery* or *courage*. The Holy Spirit is our Comforter in the sense that He strengthens and encourages us in our struggles. The New

Testament develops at least two aspects of the Spirit's comfort, based especially on Jesus' teaching:

- In the New Testament every Christian was in the Spirit, whereas in the Old Testament only selected people were led by the Spirit (for example, priests, kings, and prophets).[5]
- The New Testament stresses that the Spirit is personal. Although the Holy Spirit was personal in the Hebrew view (being "grieved," Isa. 63:10), the Spirit was usually seen as a power or energy.

31. Read John 14:16-18 in the margin. What is the relationship between a believer and the Holy Spirit? The Holy Spirit _____ with the believer and will be _____ the believer.

Identify a time when you felt comforted—strengthened or encouraged—by God's Holy Spirit.

_____

Now read 2 Corinthians 1:3-5 in the margin. How does this passage help explain why you were comforted in a time of need?

_____

Jesus promised that His Spirit would accompany His followers and would remind them of Him (see John 14:25-26). The verses you read from John promise that the Holy Spirit would remain with believers and would be in them. This relationship with the Holy Spirit allows believers to permanently possess Jesus' peace (see John 14:27), even in difficult situations, and to comfort others.

On the night of Jesus' arrest and trial, Jesus was confident that His disciples would triumph as they witnessed of Him. Read John 16:20 on page 95. Like a woman in labor, the pain would come first, then the joy of having a new child. Jesus' optimism was not a naïve cheerfulness. It was based on His imminent death and resurrection: " 'You will have suffering in this world. Be courageous! I have conquered the world' " (John 16:33). In His High Priestly prayer (see John 17) Jesus prayed for Himself and His disciples, again noting the opposition they would face (see John 17:14).

" 'I will ask the Father, and He will give you another Counselor to be with you forever. He is the Spirit of truth. The world is unable to receive Him because it doesn't see Him or know Him. But you do know Him, because He remains with you and will be in you. I will not leave you as orphans; I am coming to you.' "
John 14:16-18

"Blessed be the God and Father of our Lord Jesus Christ, the Father of mercies and the God of all comfort. He comforts us in all our affliction, so that we may be able to comfort those who are in any kind of affliction, through the comfort we ourselves receive from God. For as the sufferings of Christ overflow to us, so our comfort overflows through Christ."
2 Corinthians 1:3-5

32. Read John 17:15 and check the meaning of Jesus' prayer.
☐ **That God would protect His disciples in persecution.**
☐ **That God would exempt His disciples from persecution.**

Jesus did not ask God to exempt His disciples from suffering but to protect them as they experienced it. Jesus' confidence should encourage us as we face opposition from the world and the hurts and trials of daily life. Too often we Christians assume that because we are faithful, we should escape suffering. Following the doctrine of retribution, we assume that our piety should protect us from tragedy. Passages like these in John's Gospel remind us that Jesus and His disciples often suffered; yet they had the Holy Spirit as a constant Companion and Guide.

Christians today continue to face opposition to the gospel message we proclaim. Several years ago an International Day of Prayer for the Persecuted Church was established to help inform Christians about persecution.[6] Today Christians around the world suffer much as the first-century Christians did. Government officials arrest and torture them, and proclaiming the gospel is illegal in many places. Even in the United States, speaking the truth about Jesus Christ is becoming more difficult. But as evil intensifies in our day, Christians can rely on the Holy Spirit to give us courage and to empower our witness.

The Book of Acts highlights the Holy Spirit's role in helping the early Christians face persecution and suffering as they witnessed, established churches, and ministered. At the ascension Jesus had told the disciples, "'You will receive power when the Holy Spirit has come upon you, and you will be My witnesses in Jerusalem, in all Judea and Samaria, and to the ends of the earth'" (Acts 1:8). The Pentecost experience in Jerusalem gave these disciples boldness to begin proclaiming the gospel in Jerusalem (see Acts 4:8,31). This preaching led to persecution, but the Spirit's presence protected, empowered, and emboldened the early believers.

The Holy Spirit's leadership is evident in Paul's ministry, protecting him and empowering him to face numerous trials. The Spirit gave him courage to confront Elymas the magician (see Acts 13:9-11). After being persecuted by Jews at Antioch, Paul and Barnabas moved on, "filled with joy and with the Holy Spirit" (Acts 13:52). Occasionally, the Spirit intervened to alter Paul's itinerary

"'I assure you: You will weep and wail, but the world will rejoice. You will become sorrowful, but your sorrow will turn to joy.'"
John 16:20

"'I am not praying that You take them out of the world but that You protect them from the evil one.'"
John 17:15

(see Acts 16:6). Paul also learned from the Holy Spirit about his future suffering (see Acts 20:23; 21:10-11).

33. Check the true statements. The Spirit's presence in Paul—
☐ **exempted Paul from suffering;**
☐ **strengthened and sustained Paul in suffering;**
☐ **at times brought Paul more suffering.**

We often think that more "spiritual" people somehow escape suffering, but Paul learned that being led by the Spirit actually brought more suffering. As we will see in the next chapter, God's Spirit supported and sustained Paul in that suffering.

Our study of evil and suffering in the Gospels and in the Book of Acts has enhanced our understanding in several important ways. Most importantly, Jesus' suffering and death provide salvation for sinful humanity. His suffering was innocent, redemptive, and vicarious. Jesus' disciples are liberated from many anxieties because they know they can trust in God's love and concern for them. Christians, however, are not exempt from all suffering. Indeed, some Christians suffer specifically for living boldly for Christ in environments hostile to the gospel. Jesus had compassion on the suffering people of His day, and He encourages us to be engaged in compassionate ministry to those who suffer now. Because God's Spirit is present with us today as our Comforter, we do not suffer alone.

> **Because God's Spirit is present with us today as our Comforter, we do not suffer alone.**

---

[1] Erhard S. Gerstenberger and Wolfang Schrage, *Suffering*, trans. John E. Steely (Nashville: Abingdon, 1980), 161–62.

[2] Dietrich Bonhoeffer, *The Cost of Discipleship*, rev. ed. (New York: Macmillan, 1959), 99.

[3] G. Campbell Morgan, *The Gospel According to John* (Old Tappan, NJ: Revell, n.d.), 164–65, suggests that the punctuation of John 9:2 is misleading. If a period (rather than a comma or semicolon) were placed after *parents*, it would be clear that God did not directly cause the blindness. The original Greek would also allow such punctuation.

[4] Charles Allen Dinsmore, *Atonement in Literature and Life* (Boston: Houghton, Mifflin, and Co., 1906), 232–33.

[5] Walter Thomas Conner, *The Work of the Holy Spirit: A Treatment of the Biblical Doctrine of the Divine Spirit* (Nashville: Broadman, 1940), 33.

[6] Visit the Web site *www.persecutedchurch.org* for links to related groups.

Chapter 5

In Everything God Works for Good

Suffering in Paul's Writings

IN 1956 JIM ELLIOT, NATE SAINT, & THREE OTHERS worked together to carry the gospel to the Auca Indians of remote Ecuador. After many initial attempts to cultivate friendly relationships among the natives, the young missionaries landed their airplane on a riverside beach near the Auca community. Following days of silence from the team, a search party went in and found the bodies of the five young men. They had been impaled by Aucan spears.

Many believers wondered why God did not protect the lives of these young men who were committed to serving Him. Yet God has used their sacrifice to stir zeal in the hearts of a new generation of missionary volunteers. Many people heard the men's story and sensed God's call to be missionaries, taking a quotation from Jim's journal to heart: "He is no fool who gives up what he cannot keep to gain what he cannot lose."[1] Although the wives of the martyred missionaries had suffered from the great loss, Elisabeth Elliot

and Rachael Saint eventually carried the gospel to the Aucas themselves. Many natives came to faith in Jesus Christ. God used their
suffering to draw individuals into relationships with Him.

Paul Suffered for the Cause of Christ

The New Testament is filled with the stories of those who suffered
much yet found that God was able to work and bless through the
difficulties they faced. The Bible's account of the Apostle Paul's
ministry provides many examples of this paradox. Paul was one of
those rare individuals who suffered much, could share his experiences with others for their benefit, and could identify with the pain
of those around him.

In this chapter we will focus on Paul's experiences with suffering, and we will explore how he interpreted them. Although we
will draw on the Book of Acts as a resource for highlighting events
in his life, we will primarily focus on Paul's writings to examine his
responses to suffering and his teachings on this subject.

1. Read Paul's defense of his ministry in 2 Corinthians 11:23-27 in the margin. Underline the experience you find most startling.

Paul suffered persecution for Christ. In his early years Paul, then
known as Saul, held a high position in the Jewish religious world
and was personally responsible for the abuse and deaths of many
Christians. After Paul met the risen Jesus on the road to Damascus, the Lord previewed Paul's career to Ananias: " 'I will certainly
show him how much he must suffer for My name!' " (Acts 9:16).
In fulfillment of those words, Paul would endure a variety of painful experiences throughout his years as a missionary preacher and
teacher. The Book of Acts mentions several of these as it records his
three missionary journeys and his journey to Rome. Shortly after
Paul's conversion some Jews in Damascus plotted to kill him, and he
escaped in a basket that was lowered over the city wall at night (see
Acts 9:23-25). On the first missionary journey, Paul and Barnabas
encountered persecution in Antioch of Pisidia (see Acts 13:50). In
Iconium they received a similar hostile reaction (see Acts 14:4-6).
In Lystra Paul's preaching provoked a stoning, and he was left for
dead outside the city (see Acts 14:19).

*"Are they servants
of Christ? I'm talking
like a madman—I'm
a better one: with far
more labors, many
more imprisonments,
far worse beatings, near
death many times. Five
times I received from
the Jews 40 lashes
minus one. Three times
I was beaten with rods.
Once I was stoned.
Three times I was ship-
wrecked. I have spent
a night and a day in
the depths of the sea.
On frequent journeys,
I faced dangers from
rivers, dangers from
robbers, dangers from
my own people, dangers
from the Gentiles, dan-
gers in the city, dangers
in the open country,
dangers on the sea, and
dangers among false
brothers; labor and
hardship, many sleep-
less nights, hunger and
thirst, often without
food, cold, and lacking
clothing."*

2 Corinthians 11:23-27

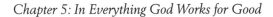

One of Paul's most famous experiences was in the Philippian jail on the second missionary journey (see Acts 16:23-39). Later on the same journey Paul and Silas were at the center of a controversy in Thessalonica (see Acts 17:5-9). Paul's preaching in Athens drew some positive response but mainly ridicule (see Acts 17:18,32-34). On the third missionary journey Paul's ministry provoked a riot in the theater of Artemis (see Acts 19:28-41).

In general, Paul's arrival in a town brought revival and/or a riot. Much of the persecution came from Jews rather than the Roman government, although Christians would eventually face persecution by Rome. As Paul traveled toward Jerusalem, he was aware that he would face trouble there as well. Yet he relentlessly continued to tell the world the good news of Jesus Christ. In response to Paul's story, we may reasonably ask, What drove Paul onward in the face of such harsh persecution?

2. Read Acts 20:22-24 in the margin. How did Paul view his life?
☐ **Unimportant compared to his task** ☐ **Unworthy**
☐ **Vital to the ministry**

What was preeminent for Paul? ☐ **Reaching Jerusalem**
☐ **Proclaiming the gospel** ☐ **Experiencing God's grace**

Read Acts 21:13-14, which is Paul's response to followers who begged him not to go to Jerusalem because of the personal risk. To what length was Paul willing to go for the sake of the gospel? ☐ **Death** ☐ **Imprisonment** ☐ **Persecution**

For Paul the mission to proclaim the gospel was preeminent. He counted his personal well-being unimportant compared to the task of sharing the good news with the world. His friends' protest broke his heart because they failed to understand the vital importance of telling people about Jesus. Nothing—not even the threat of death—could deter him from sharing the gospel.

Just as the Holy Spirit had informed Paul, his appearance in Jerusalem led to immediate persecution. When he arrived, his presence in the temple area led to a riot, his arrest, and his imprisonment. Paul then spent at least five years in prisons in Jerusalem, Caesarea,

"'I am now on my way to Jerusalem, bound in my spirit, not knowing what I will encounter there, except that in town after town the Holy Spirit testifies to me that chains and affliction are waiting for me. But I count my life of no value to myself, so that I may finish my course and the ministry I received from the Lord Jesus, to testify to the gospel of God's grace.'"
Acts 20:22-24

"Paul replied, 'What are you doing, weeping and breaking my heart? For I am ready not only to be bound, but also to die in Jerusalem for the name of the Lord Jesus.' Since he would not be persuaded, we stopped talking and simply said, 'The Lord's will be done.'"
Acts 21:13-14

and Rome awaiting a hearing before the Roman emperor. But even while jailed, Paul continued to tell others about Jesus Christ.

Even if we did not have Luke's account in Acts, Paul's letters would reveal the intensity of his suffering. Paul recounted his persecutions and sufferings for the cause of Christ to validate his authenticity as Christ's apostle and to inspire other believers to hold fast to their faith in times of trial.

> *"What has happened to me has actually resulted in the advancement of the gospel, so that it has become known throughout the whole imperial guard, and to everyone else, that my imprisonment is for Christ. Most of the brothers in the Lord have gained confidence from my imprisonment and dare even more to speak the message fearlessly."*
> Philippians 1:12-14

3. Read Philippians 1:12-14 in the margin. Who had heard that Paul was imprisoned for the sake of Christ? Underline your answer in the Scripture. What effect did Paul's imprisonment have on other Christians? Circle your answer in the Scripture.

How do you think Paul's imprisonment advanced the gospel? Check all that apply. The gospel—
☐ **had an even greater impact because of Paul's persecution;**
☐ **spread more widely as his amazing story was repeated;**
☐ **challenged other believers to adopt Paul's commitment.**
☐ **Other:** _____

Paul's suffering increased the strength of the early church while drawing the lost to Christ.

In Paul's final letter he referred to his imprisonment in a paradoxical way. Because of the gospel "I suffer, to the point of being bound like a criminal; but God's message is not bound" (2 Tim. 2:9), he proclaimed. In terms of physical pain, Paul probably preferred not to be in jail. In terms of his witness for the gospel, however, he accepted his suffering as an essential part of serving Christ in the first-century Roman world.

4. Would you be willing to endure imprisonment for the sake of the gospel? ☐ Yes ☐ No   Why?

_____

Paul suffered because of the churches' sin. Dealing with tensions and arguments in some churches also caused Paul to suffer. Paul cared for all of the churches (see 2 Cor. 11:28), but his relationships with some of them were often painful. The two letters to the church in Corinth reflect an especially strained relationship. Paul grieved over the church's rebellious attitude (see 2 Cor. 7:2-16).

5. Read 2 Corinthians 12:20-21 in the margin, in which Paul conveyed his disappointment and grief over the condition of the church in Corinth. What do you think caused Paul greater grief?
☐ **The Corinthians were embarrassing him with their behavior.**
☐ **Their behavior damaged the cause of Christ.**

What do strife and immorality in churches today communicate to unbelievers? Check all that apply.
☐ **Jesus makes no difference in people's lives.**
☐ **It's OK to keep sinning after being saved.**
☐ **These sins help churches identify with and reach the lost.**
☐ **The gospel isn't very important.**
☐ **Christians are called to be holy.**

"I fear that perhaps when I come I will not find you to be what I want, … there may by quarreling, jealousy, outbursts of anger, selfish ambitions, slander, gossip, arrogance, and disorder. I fear that when I come my God will again humiliate me in your presence, and I will grieve for many who sinned before and have not repented of the uncleanness, sexual immorality, and promiscuity they practiced."
2 Corinthians 12:20-21

No doubt the Corinthians' sins were damaging the cause of Christ and therefore distracting the church from its primary task of proclaiming the gospel. Paul often felt like a parent toward the churches he established on his missionary journeys, and like a parent, he sometimes agonized over the actions and struggles of those under his care. He wanted the Corinthians to place the same priority on the gospel as he did. Paul's zeal challenges churches today to give priority to the gospel of Jesus Christ. Churches that indulge in immorality and disputes communicate that they don't place much value on the gospel, that it's OK for believers to sin, and that Christ doesn't make a difference in believers' lives.

Paul suffered because of the rejection of the gospel. Paul was upset that the Jews were not accepting his message of salvation in Jesus Christ. Although his primary mission was to the Gentiles, Paul earnestly wanted his fellow Jews to accept Christ. If it were possible, he would forsake his salvation in order for the Jews to believe: "I speak the truth in Christ—I am not lying; my conscience is testifying to me with the Holy Spirit—that I have intense sorrow and continual anguish in my heart. For I could wish that I myself were cursed and cut off from the Messiah for the benefit of my brothers, my countrymen by physical descent" (Rom. 9:1-3).

**6. Has anyone ever rejected your witness? ☐ Yes ☐ No
If so, check the statement that describes your reaction.
☐ I was sorrowful because the person rejected Christ.
☐ I was hurt because I felt rejected.**

Paul suffered physical pain. Paul's life was scarred by a "thorn in the flesh" (see 2 Cor. 12:7). Though Paul never precisely identified this problem, scholars suggest that it might have been an ailment such as malaria or eye problems, a physical deficiency or disfigurement (see 2 Cor. 10:10), epilepsy, or chronic headaches. Whatever it was, Paul's contemporaries did not need it explained, so his letters focus not on the problem but on his response to it.

**7. Check all of the ways physical suffering can benefit believers.
☐ a. Keeps us dependent on God
☐ b. Makes us doubt God's goodness
☐ c. Keeps us humble
☐ d. Makes us more thankful for health
☐ e. Teaches us compassion for others
☐ f. Grows our faith
☐ g. Increases our patient endurance
☐ h. Teaches us that God's grace is sufficient
☐ i. Tempts us to rebel against God
☐ j. Tests our trust and reliance on God**

Paul knew that Christians could not avoid all suffering, nor should they try.

Physical ailments can help us in all of these ways except *b* and *i*. In Paul's case, the thorn reminded him of his weakness and prevented him from trying to rely on his own strength. "So that I would not exalt myself," he wrote, "a thorn in the flesh was given to me, a messenger of Satan to torment me so I would not exalt myself" (2 Cor. 12:7). Three times Paul asked God to remove the thorn, but God's response was "'My grace is sufficient for you'" (2 Cor. 12:9). Paul accepted this insight and did not continue to ask for the elimination of the thorn. He, like other Christians, learned that God would help him through the suffering instead of eliminating it. Paul knew that Christians could not avoid all suffering, nor should they try.[2] Suffering is a part of life.

8. List the four ways Paul suffered for the cause of Christ.

_____

_____

_____

_____

Go back and check the ways you also suffer for the cause of Christ. Can you honestly affirm that His grace is sufficient for you to endure this suffering? ☐ Yes ☐ No

Paul's Teachings on Suffering

Drawing on the wealth of his personal experiences of suffering and his dependence on Jesus, Paul taught believers about suffering. Paul knew that many Christians were enduring hardships and persecutions similar to those he had faced. During his ministry, which probably covered most of the middle third of the first century, Christianity was becoming more visible and vulnerable to attack. Because Paul's audiences experienced persecution, his writings focus on key topics related to suffering that still have great relevance for believers today.

Suffering Because of Sin

As a Pharisee, Paul was very knowledgeable of the Hebrew Scriptures and was familiar with the Old Testament ideas we discussed earlier in our study. Some of his letters tend to support the doctrine of retribution by clearly linking sin and suffering. Although Paul avoided a rigid application of the retributive principle, he definitely believed that sin has consequences. Paul was deeply concerned about sin's impact on human life.

> Paul was deeply concerned about sin's impact on human life.

Sin merits God's wrath. The opening chapters of Romans clearly state Paul's understanding of the relationship between sin and suffering. Paul's main argument in Romans 1–3 is that everyone is a sinner. The Gentiles were sinners, and the Jews were sinners; therefore, "all have sinned and fall short of the glory of God" (Rom. 3:23). The Gentiles experienced God's wrath because they refused to acknowledge God's revelation that was available to them in the world around them (see Rom. 1:18-25).

Three times Paul used the phrase "God delivered them over" to describe the operation of God's wrath (see Rom. 1:24,26,28). Although society's stereotype of God's wrath suggests that God is angry and sends hellfire and brimstone on the wicked, Paul taught that God often lets sinners choose the course of their lives and then allows them to experience the consequences of their choices. God has established a moral order to life that includes natural consequences for actions. In dealing with rebellious people, God merely gives them up to the destiny they choose for themselves.

"Though they knew God, they did not glorify Him as God or show gratitude. Instead, their thinking became nonsense, and their senseless minds were darkened. Therefore God delivered them over in the cravings of their hearts to sexual impurity, so that their bodies were degraded among themselves. They exchanged the truth of God for a lie, and worshiped and served something created instead of the Creator, who is blessed forever."
Romans 1:21,24-25

9. Read Romans 1:21,24-25 in the margin. When these sinners refused to worship God, what happened to their thinking? Underline your answer in the Scripture.

To what did God deliver these people? ☐ **To their enemies** ☐ **To other sinners** ☐ **To their own sinful desires**

What was the result of getting what they wanted? They were— ☐ **happy** ☐ **degraded** ☐ **killed.**

What was at the heart of their sinful action? _____

Paul instructed that God will repay people for their actions by turning them over to their own sinful desires. Idolatry was at the root of their sin. Because they exchanged God's truth for a lie, they were degraded. Whether God brings judgment in the form of wrath or natural consequences, His judgment is sure. No one can escape the penalty of sin. Indeed, God was impartial and perfectly just, not showing favoritism to the Jews over the Gentiles in retribution or in salvation (see Rom. 2:9-10; 10:12; Gal. 3:28).

Sin leads to suffering. Some of Paul's references to retribution reflect the traditional view that links suffering to sin. For example, Paul reminded the Corinthians that their lives would eventually be judged by God. Using the imagery of constructing a building on Jesus as the foundation, Paul suggested that our lives are like a building of gold, silver, precious stones, wood, hay, or straw. We will be judged and rewarded according to the kind of life we have built (see 1 Cor. 3:10-15). Occasionally, Paul listed sins and declared the penalty for such sins. He also described the eternal rewards prepared for the faithful.

10. Read 1 Corinthians 6:9-10 and Galatians 5:19-21 in the margin. Underline in the Scriptures the penalty for the sins listed.

We reap what we sow. Paul frequently applied the doctrine of retribution in general terms reminiscent of Deuteronomy or Proverbs. For instance, he wrote: "Don't be deceived: God is not mocked. For whatever a man sows he will also reap, because the one who sows to his flesh will reap corruption from the flesh, but the one who sows to the Spirit will reap eternal life from the Spirit" (Gal. 6:7-8). The context of this passage indicates that Paul was mainly concerned with our ultimate destiny, not everyday pains and grief. Rarely did Paul suggest that specific suffering here and now may be caused by the person's sin. Like the authors of Proverbs and Deuteronomy, Paul delineated two courses for life, each with concomitant consequences and rewards. He clearly showed that disobedience brings death (see Rom. 6:23) and walking in the Spirit brings life (see Rom. 8:9-11). Instead of identifying the specific cause of individual suffering, Paul taught that the penalty of sin must be paid.

11. Read Romans 2:5-10 in your Bible. What form will God's eternal judgment against the unrepentant take?
☐ **Wrath** ☐ **Hardened hearts** ☐ **Unrighteousness**

What form will God's earthly judgment against evildoers take?
☐ **Delayed judgment** ☐ **Affliction and distress** ☐ **No judgment**

What will God's eternal reward be for those who are obedient?
☐ **No accountability** ☐ **No judgment** ☐ **Eternal life**

Satan deceives and destroys. Paul understood Satan's destructive power and warned believers to avoid his insidious grip. In Romans 16:17-20 Paul urged believers to beware of people under Satanic influence who would cause divisions or create obstacles to sound teaching. He instructed his audience to remain wise about the schemes of the Evil One and reassured them that Satan's power would be crushed. Paul urgently warned believers to be alert to

"Do you not know that the unjust will not inherit God's kingdom? Do not be deceived: no sexually immoral people, idolaters, adulterers, male prostitutes, homosexuals, thieves, greedy people, drunkards, revilers, or swindlers will inherit God's kingdom."
1 Corinthians 6:9-10

"The works of the flesh are obvious: sexual immorality, moral impurity, promiscuity, idolatry, sorcery, hatreds, strife, jealousy, outbursts of anger, selfish ambitions, dissensions, factions, envy, drunkenness, carousing, and anything similar, about which I tell you in advance—as I told you before—that those who practice such things will not inherit the kingdom of God."
Galatians 5:19-21

Satan's deception and destruction, knowing that the enemy masquerades as an angel of light (see 2 Cor. 11:13-15; 2 Thess. 2:8-12).

12. Read 2 Timothy 2:22-26 in your Bible. List righteous and unrighteous pursuits.

GODLY BEHAVIORS	UNGODLY BEHAVIORS
_____	_____
_____	_____
_____	_____
_____	_____
_____	

Look at verse 26. How are those under the enemy's influence described? _____

How is Satan's influence over them described? _____

Paul described the disobedient as trapped to do Satan's will. Yet Paul also taught that sometimes God uses Satan to test believers' faith or to bring God's punishment. For example, in 1 Corinthians 5:5 Paul encouraged the church to discipline a sinning member by turning him "over to Satan f or the destruction of the flesh, so that his spirit may be saved in the Day of the Lord." In 1 Timothy 1:19-20 Paul again referred to Satan's role in God's punishment of Hymenaeus and Alexander, who had "suffered the shipwreck of their faith" and were guilty of blasphemy. In these contexts Paul pointed to Satan's formidable power but clearly taught that Satan was under God's authority and had to operate within God's boundaries. Those who sin have at least temporarily identified themselves with Satan and will suffer the consequences of that loyalty.

Christ saves us from the suffering caused by sin. To explain that God extends hope to sinners, Paul contrasted Adam and Christ, portrayed as the second Adam (see Rom. 5:12-21).

13. Read Romans 5:18-19 in the margin. Whose disobedience brought condemnation on humanity? _____
Whose obedience provided justification for humanity? _____

"As through one trespass there is condemnation for everyone, so also through one righteous act there is life-giving justification for everyone. For just as through one man's disobedience the many were made sinners, so also through the one man's obedience the many will be made righteous."
Romans 5:18-19

Adam's sin brought sin and death into human history, while Christ's obedience provided the avenue of salvation. Paul taught that Adam's disobedience introduced sin and its consequences into the world, but Christ introduced salvation and its eternal rewards. By asking forgiveness for their sins and placing faith in Christ, people can be delivered from the eternal consequences of sin.

14. Review Paul's teachings on the link between sin and suffering by underlining the correct word or phrase in each pair.

a. Everyone is (innocent, a sinner) and deserves God's (reward, wrath).

b. God responds to rebellion by (turning people over to the consequences of their choices, ignoring it).

c. Paul affirmed the doctrine of retribution by teaching that sin has (consequences, universal appeal).

d. Paul emphasized that disobedience brings (success, death), while walking in the Spirit brings (life, understanding).

e. Paul emphasized sin's (eternal consequences, earthly effects).

f. Paul warned believers of Satan's ability to (deceive and destroy, enlighten and embolden).

g. The solution to the sin that causes suffering is (superior wisdom, forgiveness through Christ).

Paul reminds us that the pervasive cause of human suffering is sin. Often we attribute contemporary social problems to sociological, psychological, and economic causes, but Paul identified the root of these social problems. Paul's primary concern was that sin breaks a relationship with God. Without Christ we are "slaves of sin" (Rom. 6:17). Our bondage to sin necessarily leads to problems in this life and ultimately to punishment from God. Only Christ can deliver people from the suffering caused by sin.

> Only Christ can deliver people from the suffering caused by sin.

Suffering for the Gospel

Being a Christian in the first century was dangerous because both the Jews and the Roman government persecuted believers. Christians encountered opposition in the basic societal relationships of home, state, and church. Anticipating these injustices, Paul wrote from prison: "Don't be ashamed of the testimony about our Lord, or of me His prisoner. Instead, share in suffering for the gospel, relying on the power of God" (2 Tim. 1:8). He encouraged believers to face unjust suffering courageously in God's power and not to be ashamed of their Lord. Paul emphasized that Christians' persecution was not a result of wrongdoing but a testimony to their righteousness. Believers would be persecuted as Jesus had been.

Suffering at home. Relationships in the home had the potential to bring suffering to believers. Because only some family members might be Christians, they might be mistreated by non-Christian members. Therefore, Paul discouraged Christians from marrying non-Christians (see 2 Cor. 6:14). Acknowledging that occasionally only one spouse would become a believer, he encouraged Christian spouses to remain married to unbelieving husbands or wives because of the positive impact they could have on the nonbeliever. If the non-Christian wanted to break the relationship, the believer should not despair (see 1 Cor. 7:12-16). The Christian spouse, however, should not initiate the divorce.

Discussing family relationships, Paul emphasized loving submission, not domination (see Eph. 5:21). He especially stressed that the husband should love his wife and should "not be harsh" with her (Col. 3:19, NIV). Paul also encouraged fathers to care for their children without provoking them (see Col. 3:21; Eph. 6:4). He warned Christian slaves, then considered part of the family, not to disrespect their masters (see 1 Tim. 6:1). If their masters were not Christians, slaves could witness to them through their behavior.

"… submitting to one another in the fear of Christ."
Ephesians 5:21

15. How can godly relationships in Christian families form a basis for witnessing to unbelieving family members?

_____

_____

How can ungodly relationships in Christian families ruin a witness to unbelieving family members?

_____

_____

In spite of opposition, believers can possibly win their families to Christ through their godly behavior and witness. Paul made it clear that a believing family member was not to show disrespect to unbelieving ones. He was concerned that new converts might immediately change their family relationships. Women, for example, might assume that they no longer needed to be concerned about their non-Christian husbands' advice. Flaunting her Christian freedom, a wife might bring unnecessary suffering on herself and her family. A Christian slave might stop obeying his non-Christian master's orders, bringing serious penalties on himself and sowing discord in the household. Paul taught submission in these domestic relationships (see Eph. 5:22-28; Col. 3:18,22).

Suffering because of the state. Paul knew that Christians might face suffering from the state authorities. As we have already seen, Jews and Romans often persecuted the early believers, but Paul still instructed believers to have an attitude of submission and obey the authorities, including paying taxes (see Rom. 13:1-7). Although Paul did not condone all of the Roman Empire's policies, such as emperor worship, he wanted to remind Christians that they should strive to be exemplary citizens. He even encouraged believers to pray for their political leaders (see 1 Tim. 2:1-2).

When Christians face a conflict between their beliefs and the laws of the state, many lean heavily on the principle of obeying God rather than people (see Acts 5:29). Obedience to God sometimes brings you into a conflict with the state. For this reason a believer's choice to obey God needs to include a readiness to suffer the consequences. Throughout the world today Christians suffer severe persecution and even death for the cause of Christ. In some places a person who converts to follow Christ may become an outcast or may be executed. Often pastors and lay people are beaten, arrested, and jailed for preaching the gospel or sharing their faith.

> A believer's choice to obey God needs to include a readiness to suffer the consequences.

16. Read Romans 13:1-7 in your Bible and check the correct statements of Paul's teachings.
☐ Be careful not to express your faith in public.
☐ Submit to government authority.
☐ Pay taxes.
☐ Take up arms against the government when you disagree.

Paul taught believers to submit to government authority and to pay taxes. Today as America's believers are increasingly discouraged from publicly expressing our faith, we must be faithful to take a stand for Christ and to suffer if necessary. Former Alabama Chief Justice Roy Moore was removed from office for insisting that the state has a right to acknowledge God and His sovereignty. Like Paul, Moore was willing to suffer the consequences. He lost his position, but God used his testimony to inspire other believers to take a stand for God in their culture.

Suffering in the church. Paul realized that Christians could create suffering for one another by embracing evil. Misunderstanding and jealousy, for example, might cause divisions among believers. Corinth is a classic example of a church with many internal problems caused by sin. The Corinthians had taken sides and had formed four rival groups (see 1 Cor. 1:12). Paul was very upset by their disunity, pointing to it as evidence of these believers' immaturity (see 1 Cor. 3:1-4). Some Corinthian Christians had even resorted to trying to settle their differences by taking lawsuits before pagan judges (see 1 Cor. 6:1-8).

17. Read 1 Corinthians 6:7. What did Paul recommend?

_____

"It is already a total defeat for you that you have lawsuits against one another. Why not rather put up with injustice? Why not rather be cheated?"
1 Corinthians 6:7

Paul suggested that believers would have a better witness to a non-Christian society if they were willing to endure suffering. In other passages he acknowledged that Christians have certain rights as citizens, but he encouraged believers to waive those rights in order to have an effective witness to others. For example, Paul taught that eating food offered to idols was permissible, but to avoid offending someone who believed it was wrong, he instructed them to give up that food: "If food causes my brother to fall, I will never again eat meat, so that I won't cause my brother to fall" (1 Cor. 8:13).

"We endure everything so that we will not hinder the gospel of Christ. Although I am free from all people, I have made myself a slave to all, in order to win more people."
1 Corinthians 9:12,19

18. Read 1 Corinthians 9:12,19 in the margin. For what purpose did Paul inhibit his own freedom?

_____

Paul noted that he had certain rights as an apostle, but he did not exercise these rights if they hindered his ability to share the gospel (see 1 Cor. 9:4-7,12,15-19). He made himself a slave to others in order to win them to Christ. His advice to endure injustice or a deprivation of rights is similar to Jesus' instruction to turn the other cheek and go the second mile (see Matt. 5:39-42). This teaching is critical to avoiding suffering among believers. A believer's immediate impulse might be to demand restitution or to retaliate, but in the context of Paul's world, Christians should accept injustice if the welfare of others or the integrity of their witness is at stake.

If Christians can expect unjust suffering in so many areas, why didn't Paul recommend aggressive social action to change these situations? He frequently explained that unjust suffering allows us to share in Christ's sufferings.

19. Read Romans 8:16-18. What do we receive when we share in Christ's suffering (suffer for the gospel)? ☐ A portion of Christ's glory ☐ A revelation of Christ ☐ No reward

How did Paul imply that we can endure suffering? ☐ By trying to ignore it ☐ By comparing it to heaven's gain

When believers share in Christ's suffering, they receive a portion of God's glory. We can endure suffering for the gospel by comparing it to heaven's gain.

Paul hoped his example of suffering would encourage other believers to endure their own trials. He wanted to remind them that Christ suffered and knew that believers would suffer for His name. Paul imitated Christ and challenged Christians to imitate him: "Be imitators of me, as I also am of Christ" (1 Cor. 11:1).

In one intriguing passage Paul taught that suffering as a part of the body of Christ, the church, completes Christ's suffering.

20. Read Colossians 1:24 in the margin. In each of the following statements, underline the correct word in parentheses.
a. Paul considered it a (joy, burden, surprise) to suffer for Christ.
b. When Paul spoke of Christ's body, he was referring to His (flesh, church, world).

"The Spirit Himself testifies together with our spirit that we are God's children, and if children, also heirs—heirs of God and co-heirs with Christ—seeing that we suffer with Him so that we may also be glorified with Him. For I consider that the sufferings of this present time are not worth comparing with the glory that is going to be revealed to us."
Romans 8:16-18

"I rejoice in my sufferings for you, and I am completing in my flesh what is lacking in Christ's afflictions for His body, that is, the church."
Colossians 1:24

c. Paul explained that although Christ's physical afflictions have ended, suffering for His cause will (continue, end, be delayed).

d. Paul wanted believers to know that the church must suffer in order to make known (Christ's afflictions, Paul's role in the church, God's message—the gospel).

Paul was not saying that Christ's suffering was inadequate for our salvation. Paul knew that the same world that hated Christ would hate the church and would direct that hatred toward His faithful body. Later Paul often used the word picture of the church as the body of Christ (see 1 Cor. 12). Whatever happens to one part of the body affects all of the body: "If one member suffers, all the members suffer with it" (1 Cor. 12:26). Paul taught that suffering an injustice for the sake of the gospel has a direct impact on the entire community of faith and continues the suffering ministry of Christ Himself. You should have answered *a. joy, b. church, c. continue,* and *d. God's message—the gospel.*

Suffering an injustice for the sake of the gospel continues the suffering ministry of Christ.

21. Check ways you would be willing to suffer for the gospel.
☐ **Be rejected by your family**
☐ **Lose your job for witnessing**
☐ **Endure ridicule for standing for Christ**
☐ **Alter your routine to spend time with a lost person**
☐ **Witness door to door**
☐ **Swallow your pride and refuse to retaliate or justify yourself**
☐ **Spend time in ministry**
☐ **Use vacation time to go on a mission trip**
☐ **Other:** _____

Death and Suffering
In chapter 2 we saw that Adam and Eve's choice to sin resulted in the inevitability of death for all humanity. Each day death causes great suffering for people everywhere. Many who are close to death naturally fear losing their lives. Survivors grieve over losing their loved ones and might worry about losing others.

22. Check emotions you experienced after a loved one's death.
☐ **Guilt** ☐ **Anger** ☐ **Fear** ☐ **Worry** ☐ **Grief** ☐ **Bitterness**

Paul, who frequently wrote about this subject, identified two kinds of death. In some contexts he clearly pointed to physical death. In other contexts he referred to spiritual death—someone's condition without Christ (see Eph. 2:1; 1 Tim. 5:6). We will focus on Paul's view of physical death in order to address the suffering it causes.

Paul looked at physical death from three perspectives.

Death is destruction. When people die, their everyday relationships with friends and relatives are broken. Death causes grief for those who are left behind. A dying person may be apprehensive about death because of the mystery that seems to surround the event. When this aspect of death is emphasized, death is seen as an enemy: "The last enemy to be abolished is death" (1 Cor. 15:26).

Death is departure. Paul viewed death as an entry to the next life.

23. Read Philippians 1:21,23 and 2 Timothy 4:6-7 in the margin. Paul's view of death seems to be one of ☐ fear ☐ hope ☐ confusion.   Why do you think Paul viewed death this way?

_____

"For me, living is Christ and dying is gain. I have the desire to depart and be with Christ—which is far better."
Philippians 1:21,23

Paul's sense of fulfillment about his ministry and his assurance of a closer relationship with Christ after death prompted his yearning for death. Paul knew that apart from Christ there is no such hope, and in some letters he offered pastoral advice to mourners.

"The time for my departure is close. I have fought the good fight, I have finished the race, I have kept the faith."
2 Timothy 4:6-7

24. Read 1 Thessalonians 4:13-18 in your Bible. Indicate whether these statements are true (T) or false (F).
____ **a. Christians don't have to grieve over a believer's death.**
____ **b. A Christian's hope is based on Christ's resurrection.**
____ **c. When Christ returns, some believers will be dead; others will be living.**
____ **d. When Christ returns, believers who are living will be taken up first.**
____ **e. Confidence in Christ's return comforts and encourages.**

The correct answers are a. F, b. T, c. T, d. F, e. T. Go back and circle the truth that is particularly encouraging to you.

Death is defeated. In 2 Timothy 1:10 Paul described Jesus as the One "who has abolished death and has brought life and immortality to light through the gospel." Paul was not implying that Christians are exempt from physical death but that Christians have a new kind of life that transcends ordinary human life and death. Christ's death and resurrection transformed the meaning of death for Christians. Paul depicted death as the last enemy because Christ is the triumphant Lord (see 1 Cor. 15:20-28). Jesus' resurrection was the firstfruits of the resurrection of all people. Returning to his comparison of Adam and Christ, Paul suggested that whereas Adam brought death (see 1 Cor. 15:21), Jesus is the "life-giving spirit" (1 Cor. 15:45).

> "Death has been
> swallowed up
> in victory.
> O Death, where
> is your victory?
> O Death, where
> is your sting?"
> 1 Corinthians 15:54-55

25. Read 1 Corinthians 15:54-55 in the margin. Why don't Christians need to fear death?

_____

The victory over death is already ours. Jesus' resurrection ensures our eternal existence with God.

Paul's writings dealt with physical death realistically and hopefully. Christians can confront physical death—ours and others'—with confidence in the God of hope. The God who raised Jesus from the dead gives us hope to endure suffering and face death confidently. Because Jesus lives, we too will live.

Suffering from Demonic Attack

When Paul described the struggles that Christians face, he looked beyond conflicts among people. He knew that some suffering comes from demonic attack. After describing Satan's role in the fall of humanity, the Hebrews did not discuss the Devil, demons, or angels in any depth until apocalyptic literature became prominent. But Jesus often spoke of the Devil and demons, and we saw that Jesus frequently performed exorcisms.

Paul also attributed some suffering to the activity of demons and the Devil, the evil spiritual forces that oppose God, His people, and His purposes. From Paul's discussions of these supernatural beings, we can learn two things about evil and suffering.

Evil forces have been defeated. Paul taught that God is omnipotent (all-powerful) and Satan is not. Apart from Christ a person may be controlled or dominated by evil, but a Christian doesn't need to fear these forces (see Eph. 2:1-5). Indeed, one of Paul's favorite images for the victory in Jesus' death and resurrection was a military one. Jesus has utterly and completely defeated Satan's forces. Through Christ's death and resurrection God "disarmed the rulers and authorities and disgraced them publicly; He triumphed over them by Him" (Col. 2:15). This word picture refers to a conqueror leading his vanquished foes through the city streets in a victory procession.

26. What does Jesus' victory mean for believers?
☐ **Beware because Satan can still win the war.**
☐ **Satan and his demons are defeated.**
☐ **Believers don't need to fear Satan.**
☐ **All spiritual battles have ended.**

Because Christ was victorious, Satan and his demons are already defeated foes, and Christians need not fear them. As we saw in chapter 4, however, some struggles may continue even though the major battle is won. Christ has defeated Satan, but Satan is still fighting for a lost cause. Thus, Paul warned Christians about the work of demonic beings in our lives (see 2 Cor. 10:3-4; Eph. 6:12).

Christians should prepare for spiritual battle. Knowing that the struggle with Satan would continue for a while, Paul called Christians to battle. His most powerful passage encourages believers to put on "the full armor of God" (Eph. 6:11,13; also see 1 Thess. 5:8). By putting on truth, righteousness, the gospel of peace, faith, salvation, and the Word of God, Christians are prepared to withstand the enemy's attacks and to wage spiritual battles.

27. Read Ephesians 6:14-17. What can Christians do with the spiritual armor? Check all that apply. ☐ **Engage the enemy in battle** ☐ **Thwart the enemy's schemes** ☐ **Escape the war**

In what spiritual battles will the armor be effective? Underline your answer in the Scripture.

"Stand, therefore, with truth like a belt around your waist, righteousness like armor on your chest, and your feet sandaled with readiness for the gospel of peace. In every situation take the shield of faith, and with it you will be able to extinguish the flaming arrows of the evil one. Take the helmet of salvation, and the sword of the Spirit, which is God's word."
Ephesians 6:14-17

Spiritual armor, available only to believers because of the Holy Spirit's presence in us, equips us to engage the enemy and to thwart the enemy's schemes in every spiritual battle.

Paul was confident that although Christians will experience trouble in this life, their victory is assured. The victory, however, does not ultimately depend on human action. The real assurance of victory over demonic forces is God Himself.

28. Read Romans 8:37-39 in the margin. Through Christ we are more than _____.

"In all these things we are more than victorious through Him who loved us. For I am persuaded that neither death nor life, nor angels nor rulers, nor things present, nor things to come, nor powers, nor height, nor depth, nor any other created thing will have the power to separate us from the love of God that is in Christ Jesus our Lord!"
Romans 8:37-39

Responding to Suffering

Paul taught believers that they could live victoriously through suffering. Unfortunately, many people find it difficult to live in victory when trials come their way. Imagine that two believers have similar car accidents. Both lose a leg, but they react differently to their new circumstances. The first person moves from his initial shock at the loss of his limb to a state of bitterness. He resists any kind of physical therapy and begins to lose faith in God. The second person is also shocked by her loss, but she eventually enters rehabilitation and learns how to walk with an artificial leg. Although she questions why God allowed the accident to happen, she responds hopefully to her future and places her trust in Him. These scenarios illustrate that although all people experience suffering, we can choose the way we will respond to it. Suffering can make us bitter and skeptical, or it can lead us to deeper faith and trust.

We have learned in this chapter that Paul suffered intensely for the cause of Christ. Yet in every situation he learned to rely on Christ's power, to boast in his inadequacies so that Christ could be powerful in him, and to rejoice in the midst of his trials. Even while suffering, Paul boldly, courageously, and relentlessly proclaimed the gospel of Jesus Christ. He provides a steadfast role model for Christians today. His encouragement rings as true to us now as it did to the early Christian church:

- Rejoice in suffering (see Rom. 5:3).
- Be patient in affliction (see Rom. 12:12).
- Don't repay evil for evil (see Rom. 12:17).
- Be filled with encouragement (see 2 Cor. 7:4).
- Be content in all circumstances (see Phil. 4:11).

• Recognize that God will supply all our needs according to His riches in glory through Christ Jesus (see Phil. 4:19).

The unwavering faith that Paul so passionately lived and taught begs the questions, What gave Paul his bold assurance and confident strength in light of his suffering? How can we face suffering with that kind of faith?

29. Read Philippians 3:7-10 in the margin. Underline each reason for Paul's sustaining strength. Read Philippians 4:11-12 in the margin. What had Paul's suffering taught him? To be _____ in spite of his circumstances.

When Paul said in Philippians 4:11-12 that he had learned how to be content, he emphasized reliance on God rather than self-sufficiency. His contentment was based on his faith in God, not on his emotional state. He added, "I am able to do all things through Him who strengthens me" (Phil. 4:13). Concluding this same letter, he wrote, "My God will supply all your needs according to His riches in glory in Christ Jesus" (Phil. 4:19; also see 1 Tim. 6:6-8). Paul was content in his suffering because of the God he trusted. Paul's writings identify three ways we can claim that contentment.

Place your hope in God. In Paul's letters to the Thessalonian Christians, Paul addressed their perplexity about the deaths of loved ones and the apparent delay of Christ's return. The Thessalonians were not to grieve "like the rest, who have no hope" (1 Thess. 4:13). Christ would return, and they would reunite with their loved ones, though perhaps not on the Thessalonians' timetable. Paul reminded these Christians that their circumstances were not hopeless. Although they were suffering from loss and persecution, God would punish their persecutors (see 2 Thess. 1:4-12). He would encourage and strengthen them in their struggles.

30. Read 2 Thessalonians 2:16-17 in the margin on page 118. Identify the Thessalonians' source of hope.
☐ **Good works** ☐ **God** ☐ **The legal system**

Paul was confident that the Thessalonians could endure suffering if they placed their trust in God.

"I also consider everything to be a loss in view of the surpassing value of knowing Christ Jesus my Lord. Because of Him I have suffered the loss of all things and consider them filth, so that I may gain Christ and be found in Him. My goal is to know Him and the power of His resurrection and the fellowship of His sufferings, being conformed to His death."
Philippians 3:7-10

"I have learned to be content in whatever circumstances I am. I know both how to have a little, and I know how to have a lot. In any and all circumstances I have learned the secret of being content—whether well-fed or hungry, whether in abundance or in need."
Philippians 4:11-12

Look to God for comfort. Paul's correspondence with Corinth reveals his personal struggles and his faith in God's help. Several times he indicated that "God is faithful" (1 Cor. 1:9; also see 10:13; 2 Cor. 1:18). Although temptations and tests come our way, God provides a way of escape so that we can bear it (see 1 Cor. 10:13). Confident in God's provision, Paul proclaimed to the Corinthians that God is "the Father of mercies and the God of all comfort. He comforts us in all our affliction" (2 Cor. 1:3-4). God identifies with us in our suffering, and He helps us.

31. Copy the definition of *comfort* from page 21: _____

_____

Read 2 Corinthians 4:1 in the margin. What did God give Paul to strengthen him for ministry? _____

As we have seen before, *comfort* originally meant *to strengthen or encourage*, not merely to console in a sentimental sense. Because of the strengthening mercy God showed him, Paul did not give up in difficult moments. Relying on God's power, he was able to endure his problems: "We are pressured in every way but not crushed; we are perplexed but not in despair; we are persecuted but not abandoned; we are struck down but not destroyed" (2 Cor. 4:8-9). Paul relied on the God of all comfort. Whether that comfort came in human form or through divine intervention, Paul acknowledged that God was its source.

32. Name persons God uses to provide you comfort and support.

_____

Stop and thank God for them.

Believe that God works for your good. In the first century the Roman Christians were in danger because of the threat of persecution. In the Book of Romans Paul wanted to encourage them as they faced adversity.

33. Read the verses in the margin and fill in the blanks.
a. Romans 5:3: _____ in affliction.
b. Romans 5:3-4: Affliction produces _____.
   Endurance produces _____ _____.
   Proven character produces _____.
c. Romans 12:12: Rejoice in _____. Be _____
   in affliction.
d. Romans 12:19: Do not seek _____.
e. Romans 15:5: God is the God of _____
   and _____.
f. Romans 15:13: God gives _____ and _____.

Although suffering is painful, Paul taught, it shapes a believer's character (see Rom. 5:3-5). Realizing that Roman Christians might be tempted to retaliate against their persecutors, Paul echoed Jesus' teaching on rejecting vindictiveness and leaving vengeance to God alone (see Rom. 12:14-21). He encouraged Roman Christians to be patient in their suffering, even to rejoice in it (see Rom. 5:3; 12:12). God would help them in their suffering. The "God of endurance and encouragement" is also the "God of hope" (Rom. 15:5,13).

Paul's most famous statement on God's relationship to suffering is probably Romans 8:28: "We know that in all things God works for the good of those who love him, who have been called according to his purpose" (NIV). In chapter 1 we saw that this verse doesn't mean that God directly causes all suffering. Rather, it points to divine omnicompetence. No matter what situation we might face, our struggles are not beyond God's ultimate control. In spite of tremendous evil and suffering in a situation, God can still help us.

The context of this famous verse is important. In describing the Christian's life, Paul contrasted flesh and Spirit. A Christian lives according to the Spirit, experiencing "life and peace" (Rom. 8:6). But Paul reminds us that Christians will also suffer. Salvation does not exempt us from hurt. We are "heirs of God and co-heirs with Christ—seeing that we suffer with Him" (Rom. 8:17). Paul pinpointed a basic paradox of the Christian life: Christians have peace; yet they suffer! However, we should compare these sufferings with our future freedom from suffering (see Rom. 8:29-30). Our earthly trials may be intense, but God's ability to help us is stronger. Nothing can separate us from His love (see Rom. 8:35-39).

"We also rejoice in our afflictions, because we know that affliction produces endurance, endurance produces proven character, and proven character produces hope."
Romans 5:3-4

"Rejoice in hope; be patient in affliction."
Romans 12:12

"Do not avenge yourselves; instead, leave room for His wrath. For it is written: Vengeance belongs to Me; I will repay, says the Lord."
Romans 12:19

"May the God of endurance and encouragement grant you agreement with one another, according to Christ Jesus."
Romans 15:5

"May the God of hope fill you with all joy and peace in believing."
Romans 15:13

34. Read Romans 8:35-39 in your Bible. How does this passage encourage you as you face trials, pain, evil, and suffering?

_____

_____

_____

Throughout his ministry Paul's ability to see his own suffering in the context of God's love, power, and plans for the future enabled him to rejoice. He tried to comfort others with his insight and faith. Paul's final letter expressed confidence that even when others deserted him, God would stand by him: "The Lord will rescue me from every evil work and will bring me safely into His heavenly kingdom. To Him be the glory forever and ever!" (2 Tim. 4:18).

That attitude strengthened the early church and still encourages believers today. According to early Christian tradition, Paul was executed as a martyr. Although he did not escape prison and death, he was able to understand his suffering within the context of his Christian faith. No matter how we suffer, Paul reassured us that God is with us in our suffering and that our suffering unites us with Jesus Christ. We do not suffer alone.

We do not suffer alone.

**35. Think about the pain and suffering you experience.
Do you—**

place your hope in God?	☐ **Sometimes**	☐ **Usually**	☐ **Always**
look to God for comfort?	☐ **Sometimes**	☐ **Usually**	☐ **Always**
believe that God works for your good?	☐ **Sometimes**	☐ **Usually**	☐ **Always**

Pray and ask God to help you seek Him when you suffer.

---

[1] Elisabeth Elliot, _Shadow of the Almighty: The Life and Testament of Jim Elliot_ (New York: Harper and Brothers, 1958), 15.

[2] Merrill Proudfoot, _Suffering: A Christian Understanding_ (Philadelphia: Westminster, 1964), 51.

Chapter 6

Suffering with Christ
Suffering in the General Letters and Revelation

BEING A CHRISTIAN ALWAYS INVOLVES RISK. In A.D. 155 Christianity was illegal in the Roman Empire. Although some believers denied their faith in Jesus in order to live, Polycarp, the elderly bishop of Smyrna, steadfastly testified to his beliefs. The Roman officials offered him opportunities to go free if he would swear by the emperor and curse Christ. But Polycarp replied: "Eighty-six years I have served him, and he never did me any wrong. How can I blaspheme my King who saved me?"[1] Being faithful to Jesus cost Polycarp his life.

As Christianity grew numerically and geographically, it became increasingly visible in the Roman Empire. Although the government usually allowed a conquered nation to practice its native religion, new religions were illegal. At first the Romans saw Christianity as a new sect or splinter group within Judaism (see Acts 18:12-16) and overlooked it. Later, however, it became obvious to the Romans that Christianity was different and potentially dangerous. At that point proclaiming Christ became a hazard.

General Letters
Hebrews, James, 1–2 Peter, 1–3 John, and Jude. (The views of suffering in 2 Peter and Jude are so similar that we will not examine Jude separately.)

In this chapter we will look at several New Testament writings that reflect the suffering created by increasing opposition to Christianity. The General Letters—Hebrews, James, 1–2 Peter, 1–3 John, and Jude—are so named because the original audiences were not as clearly defined as those in Paul's letters. We will also explore the insights of Revelation, an apocalyptic book, into suffering. Because the writers and their audiences experienced suffering, these books teach us what it means to suffer for Christ and to remain faithful to Him in an environment of persecution and disbelief.

Suffering in the Book of Hebrews

The Jewish Christians who were addressed in the Book of Hebrews faced a dilemma. Threatened with persecution, they were tempted to publicly deny their Christian commitment and return to the safer position of being a Jew. For this reason the major doctrinal theme of Hebrews is the superiority of Christianity over Judaism. The writer gave Jewish converts to Christianity practical guidance for enduring suffering while holding fast to their faith in Christ.

"We have a great deal to say about this, and it's difficult to explain, since you have become slow to understand. For though by this time you ought to be teachers, you need someone to teach you again the basic principles of God's revelation. You need milk, not solid food. Now everyone who lives on milk is inexperienced with the message about righteousness, because he is an infant. But solid food is for the mature—for those whose senses have been trained to distinguish between good and evil."
Hebrews 5:11-14

Go on to maturity. The writer of Hebrews was concerned that his audience would go backward rather than forward in their Christian walk. At a time when they should have been maturing as Christians, the Jewish believers were still spiritual babies (see Heb. 5:11-14). The author admonished them to "go on to maturity" (Heb. 6:1), using Old Testament examples to make his point. The Hebrews at the time of the Exodus, for example, should have followed God's leadership and entered the promised land, but they rebelled and did not find rest in Canaan (see Heb. 3:7-19). Therefore, Christians who remained faithful to God during the current adversity would find rest, while the faithless would not (see Heb. 4:1-11).

1. Read Hebrews 5:11-14 in the margin. List qualities of mature and immature believers in the blanks.

MATURE BELIEVERS	IMMATURE BELIEVERS
_____	_____
_____	_____
_____	_____
_____	_____

Why is spiritual maturity critical for Christians facing trials?

Do you have the spiritual maturity to face adversity without denying your faith? ☐ **Yes** ☐ **No**

Believers who press on to spiritual maturity in Christ are better equipped to stand firm in the face of opposition.

Exercise faith. In chapter 11 the author encouraged the Jewish believers to build their faith. He gave a roll call of Hebrew heroes and heroines, using their testimonies to demonstrate what faith really is. Faith is proof of the unseen (see Heb. 11:1) that manifests itself in courageous action in the face of opposition. Moses, for example, chose to identify with the Hebrew slaves rather than enjoy the pleasures of Pharaoh's palace: "He considered reproach for the sake of the Messiah to be greater wealth than the treasures of Egypt" (Heb. 11:26). Throughout chapter 11 the author named several Old Testament figures who exercised their faith in similar ways, trusting in eventual blessings for their steadfast commitment. Sometimes he stressed their victory over the opposition (see Heb. 11:33-35a), but elsewhere he stressed the suffering without noting the victory (see Heb. 11:35b-38). This same "cloud of witnesses" (Heb. 12:1), the writer taught, surrounded the first-century Christians, observing their response to suffering.

2. Read Hebrews 12:1-2 in the margin. Who or what is the object of our faith? ☐ **Our strength and stamina** ☐ **Jesus** ☐ **Our spoken word of faith**

Our faith is anchored in Jesus. Placing our faith in Him enables us to endure suffering in His strength.

Rely on Christ's power. Jesus' example for the first-century believers was even more important than the examples of the Hebrew faithful. Jesus endured great suffering for God's greater purposes. If Christians could learn to follow Jesus' example as "the source and

"Faith is the reality of what is hoped for, the proof of what is not seen." Hebrews 11:1

"Since we also have such a large cloud of witnesses surrounding us, let us lay aside every weight and the sin that so easily ensnares us, and run with endurance the race that lies before us, keeping our eyes on Jesus, the source and perfecter of our faith, who for the joy that lay before Him endured a cross and despised the shame, and has sat down at the right hand of God's throne." Hebrews 12:1-2

perfecter of our faith, who for the joy that lay before Him endured a cross" (Heb. 12:2), they would be able to endure any trial.

Jesus is not only our example but also our source of strength when we suffer. First, Jesus' suffering allowed Him to understand the suffering of people: "Since He Himself was tested and has suffered, He is able to help those who are tested" (Heb. 2:18).

"We do not have a high priest who is unable to sympathize with our weaknesses, but One who has been tested in every way as we are, yet without sin. Therefore let us approach the throne of grace with boldness, so that we may receive mercy and find grace to help us at the proper time."
Hebrews 4:15-16

3. Read Hebrews 4:15-16 in the margin. Because Jesus suffered as we do, what does He provide for us when we need help?

_____

When we suffer, we can rely on Jesus to give us mercy and grace to endure. Furthermore, we can have confidence in the outcome of our trials because Jesus' crucifixion and resurrection defeated two causes of suffering, the Devil and death (see Heb. 2:14-15).

Accept God's discipline. Christians should also expect to suffer because of God's discipline. Using a parent-child analogy, the author said that children should expect to be disciplined. Only illegitimate children avoided suffering, presumably because no one really cared about them. Unlike the Jewish Christians' persecutors, God really cared for His people and disciplined them from love.

4. Read Hebrews 12:5-11 in the margin on page 125. How does God's discipline benefit a Christian? Choose the best answer.
☐ It proves that God loves His children.
☐ It proves that a believer is a child of God.
☐ It enables a believer to share in God's holiness.
☐ It causes a believer to respect God.

What fruit does God's discipline bring to a believer's life?
_____ **and** _____

Name something you have learned from God's discipline.

_____

God's discipline benefits us by enabling us to share in His holiness. His discipline yields the fruit of peace and righteousness.

Be assured of God's presence. The writer assured the Jewish Christians that although they suffered, they had God's help: "I will never leave you or forsake you. Therefore, we may boldly say:

> *The Lord is my helper;*
> *I will not be afraid.*
> *What can man do to me?"* Hebrews 13:5-6

This reminder promises believers that we never suffer alone. In the face of suffering, we experience God's presence.

5. According to Hebrews, how should believers respond to persecution?
☐ **Exercise faith.**   ☐ **Deny Christ.**
☐ **Fight back.**   ☐ **Rely on Christ's power.**
☐ **Become bitter.**   ☐ **Be assured of God's presence.**

Suffering in the Book of James
The Book of James was also written to strengthen persecuted believers. James gave very specific advice to those who suffered.

Recognize the source of your suffering. James warned believers not to blame God for all of their suffering: "No one undergoing a trial should say, 'I am being tempted by God.' For God is not tempted by evil, and He Himself doesn't tempt anyone" (Jas. 1:13). Temptation doesn't come from God. Instead, James said that temptation is connected with a desire that eventually leads to sin: "Each person is tempted when he is drawn away and enticed by his own evil desires. Then after desire has conceived, it gives birth to sin, and when sin is fully grown, it gives birth to death" (Jas. 1:14-15).

6. Is Satan always the source of temptation? ☐ Yes ☐ No
What is an additional source? _____

Satan is not always the source of temptation. Our evil desires also tempt us to sin.

"My son, do not take the Lord's discipline lightly, or faint when you are reproved by Him; for the Lord disciplines the one He loves, and punishes every son whom He receives. Endure it as discipline: God is dealing with you as sons. For what son is there whom a father does not discipline? But if you are without discipline—which all receive—then you are illegitimate children and not sons. Furthermore, we had natural fathers discipline us, and we respected them. Shouldn't we submit even more to the Father of spirits and live? For they disciplined us for a short time based on what seemed good to them, but He does it for our benefit, so that we can share His holiness. No discipline seems enjoyable at the time, but painful. Later on, however, it yields the fruit of peace and righteousness to those who have been trained by it."
Hebrews 12:5-11

Even though God does not tempt us, He often tests us. In fact, James interpreted his readers' suffering in light of the testing of their faith.

"'The LORD your God is testing you to know whether you love the LORD your God with all your heart and all your soul.'"
Deuteronomy 13:3

7. Read the passages in the margin and match the references with the reasons God tests believers.

____ 1. Deuteronomy 13:3
____ 2. Proverbs 17:3
____ 3. Luke 8:13
____ 4. 1 Thessalonians 2:4
____ 5. James 1:3

a. To approve us so that we can be entrusted with the gospel

b. To develop perseverance and maturity

c. To refine (purify) our hearts like precious metals

d. To reveal whether God's Word is rooted deeply in our hearts

e. To reveal whether we completely love God

"A crucible is for silver and a smelter is for gold, but the LORD is a tester of hearts."
Proverbs 17:3

"'The seeds on the rock are those who, when they hear, welcome the word with you. Having no root, these believe for a while and depart in a time of testing.'"
Luke 8:13

How does a believer's response to God's testing differ from a response to temptation?

_____

You should have matched the Scriptures this way: 1. e, 2. c, 3. d, 4. a, 5. b. While believers must reject temptation, they should submit to God's testing as a way to learn what He wants to teach them.

"Just as we have been approved by God to be entrusted with the gospel, so we speak, not to please men, but rather God, who examines our hearts."
1 Thessalonians 2:4

Be patient when you suffer. When James wrote, "You also must be patient" (Jas. 5:8), he was not giving trite encouragement. James used the suffering of poor Christians at the hands of the rich to illustrate that Christians must respond to a difficult situation with patience. James supported the doctrine of retribution by using the fate of rich oppressors as an example of God's ultimate justice. The prosperity of the wicked would be temporary (see Jas. 1:11).

"The testing of your faith produces endurance."
James 1:3

8. Read James 1:2-3 in the margin on page 127. How are believers to view their suffering? _____

What is the result of this suffering? _____

James instructed the believers to see their suffering as a testing of their faith. Such testing could produce endurance. This is not passive resignation. Instead, believers look forward to a time when the Lord will return and vindicate the righteous (see Jas. 5:7-8).

9. Read James 5:7-8 in the margin. What is some precious fruit that comes from patient endurance?
☐ **Reliance on God**   ☐ **Increased faith** ☐ **Vengeance**
☐ **Strong character**   ☐ **Self-reliance**   ☐ **Hope in God's justice**

Patient endurance produces reliance on God, increased faith, strong character, and hope in God's justice. Suffering believers can place their hope in the Lord, knowing that He will make things right.

Practice an active faith. James taught believers to place their faith in God despite their circumstances (see Jas. 5:7-8). One of James's major themes was that true faith must be active. Faith without works, he taught, is dead (see Jas. 2:14-17). Believers' suffering tests our faith at a practical level. Even demons know correct ideas about God but do not have the faith evidenced by Abraham and Rahab (see Jas. 2:19-26). We must put our faith into action.

Don't be judgmental. Often when we see someone prospering unfairly, perhaps at our expense, we are inclined to become judgmental. James warned against being judgmental toward others. Read James 4:11-12 in the margin.

Don't complain. James also encouraged us not to complain, recognizing that God is the true judge (see Jas. 5:9). Complaining has terrible effects in the believer's heart and in the church.

10. What do our complaints about circumstances say to God?

_____

Circle the words that best describe problems that could grow in the body of Christ from the seeds of complaint.

| Dissatisfaction | Bitterness | Peace | Dissension |
| Resentment | Patience | Joy | Faultfinding |

"Consider it a great joy, my brothers, whenever you experience various trials, knowing that the testing of your faith produces endurance." James 1:2-3

"Be patient until the Lord's coming. See how the farmer waits for the precious fruit of the earth and is patient with it until it receives the early and the late rains. You also must be patient. Strengthen your hearts, because the Lord's coming is near." James 5:7-8

"Don't criticize one another, brothers. He who criticizes a brother or judges his brother criticizes the law and judges the law. But if you judge the law, you are not a doer of the law but a judge. There is one lawgiver and judge who is able to save and to destroy. But who are you to judge your neighbor?" James 4:11-12

When we judge others and complain, we elevate our judgment and desires above God's wisdom and plan.

Pray about your suffering. James said those who suffer must pray.

11. Read James 5:13-18 in your Bible. Check the correct statement.
☐ **Prayer ensures that our suffering will always be relieved.**
☐ **Prayer places our suffering in God's hands.**

These verses don't guarantee that every problem will be solved through prayer. Remember that Paul's thorn remained in spite of his prayer. Christians need to pray about all suffering, knowing that "the Lord is very compassionate and merciful" (Jas. 5:11), but we must recognize that miracles do not always result.

12. Which of James's teachings do you practice in suffering?
☐ **Recognize the source of your suffering.**
☐ **Be patient when you suffer.**
☐ **Don't be judgmental.**
☐ **Don't complain.**
☐ **Practice an active faith.**
☐ **Pray about your suffering.**

Circle one way you can respond to your suffering differently.

James teaches us that no matter what the source of our suffering is, a response of patient endurance shows our faith in God's ability to bring justice and relief according to His timing and His plan.

Suffering in the Books of 1–2 Peter

Peter's letters focus on two types of suffering: suffering as a Christian and suffering as an evildoer (see 1 Pet. 4:15-16). First Peter focuses on suffering as a Christian for "doing good" (1 Pet. 3:17), while 2 Peter sheds light on suffering as punishment.

First Peter: suffering for the faith. Like James, Peter saw some suffering as a test of the genuineness of faith, and he taught his readers to view their struggles in that context. Just as gold was refined by fire, their faith would be "tested by fire" (1 Pet. 1:7, NASB).

"None of you, however, should suffer as a murderer, a thief, an evildoer, or as a meddler. But if anyone suffers as a Christian, he should not be ashamed, but should glorify God with that name."
1 Peter 4:15-16

13. Read 1 Peter 4:12-14 in the margin. Sharing in the suffering of the Messiah means—
☐ **suffering a damaged reputation;**
☐ **suffering for your sins;**
☐ **suffering ridicule for the sake of the gospel.**

When we suffer for the cause of Christ, we should—
☐ **not be surprised;** ☐ **not be afraid;** ☐ **not be discouraged.**

When we are ridiculed for Christ, we are covered with—
☐ **shame;** ☐ **God's glory;** ☐ **God's peace.**

"When the fiery ordeal arises among you to test you, don't be surprised by it, as if something unusual were happening to you. Instead, as you share in the sufferings of the Messiah rejoice, so that you may also rejoice with great joy at the revelation of His glory. If you are ridiculed for the name of Christ, you are blessed, because the Spirit of glory and of God rests on you."
1 Peter 4:12-14

Though their persecution was a "fiery ordeal" that arose to test them (1 Pet. 4:12), these Christians should not be surprised by the persecution or alarmed by it. Instead, they were to rejoice that they could share in Christ's sufferings and those of other believers "throughout the world" (1 Pet. 5:9, NIV). When we suffer for Christ, we are covered with God's glory.

Peter identified two relationships in which Christians could face either direct persecution or indirect pressure to deny their faith.

- Christians risked persecution by the state. Being good citizens without denying faith presented a dilemma. Peter instructed believers to fear God and honor the emperor (see 1 Pet. 2:17).
- Christians might suffer in family relationships. Christian slaves who suffered injustice were to follow in the steps of Christ, who did not revile His persecutors (see 1 Pet. 2:21). Christian wives were to be submissive to husbands, knowing that they might be won to Christ "without words" (1 Pet. 3:1, NIV).

"Set apart the Messiah as Lord in your hearts, and always be ready to give a defense to anyone who asks you for a reason for the hope that is in you. However, do this with gentleness and respect, keeping your conscience clear, so that when you are accused, those who denounce your Christian life will be put to shame."
1 Peter 3:15-16

Peter emphasized that in all situations Christians should be prepared to offer a verbal defense to anyone who questioned them (see 1 Pet. 3:15-16). These declarations of faith should come without attempts to return evil for evil (see 1 Pet. 3:9) and without fear of the consequences (see 1 Pet. 3:14).

14. Read 1 Peter 3:15-16 in the margin. Why is it important to always be ready to defend our faith? Check all that apply.
☐ **Our testimony may be convicting to unbelievers.**
☐ **People will think twice before ridiculing us.**
☐ **We never know when a test of our faith will come.**

Why are we to respond gently and respectfully?
☐ **So that we don't malign our Christian witness**
☐ **So that we will gain the respect of our accusers**
☐ **So that we might not have to defend ourselves**

We must always be ready to defend our faith so that our testimonies will be convicting to unbelievers and because we never know when a test of our faith will come. It's important that believers respond gently and respectfully so that we don't malign our Christian witness or forfeit the opportunity to gain our accusers' respect.

Peter also advised persecuted believers to behave properly so that outsiders would be impressed (see 1 Pet. 2:12). This evangelistic motive might necessitate submission to unjust suffering.

More and more Christians today face the possibility of unjust suffering for their faith. An employee in Illinois lost her job for sharing her faith with coworkers, even though she had made sure her coworkers were willing to discuss religious issues.[2] Peter's teachings will take on more relevance as more believers are called on to suffer for their faith.

"Conduct yourselves honorably among the Gentiles, so that in a case where they speak against you as those who do evil, they may, by observing your good works, glorify God in a day of visitation."
1 Peter 2:12

15. Are you willing to lose your job for the sake of the gospel?
☐ **Yes** ☐ **No**   **Your life?** ☐ **Yes** ☐ **No**   **Are you ready to give a defense of your faith?** ☐ **No** ☐ **Sometimes** ☐ **Always**

Second Peter: suffering for false teaching. Second Peter uses the retributive principle to highlight the inevitability of God's punishment of the sinful—in this case, false teachers. In response to these teachers' actions and the problems they caused, Peter listed several Old Testament examples of wicked people whom God eventually punished (see 2 Pet. 2:4-10).

"The Day of the Lord will come like a thief; on that day the heavens will pass away with a loud noise, the elements will burn and be dissolved, and the earth and the works on it will be disclosed."
2 Peter 3:10

16. Read 2 Peter 3:10 in the margin. What solution to suffering did Peter foresee?

_____

Peter assured his readers that the Day of the Lord would come and that God's judgment would be obvious. God, he said, is always just and in charge. Those who oppose Him will be punished.

17. Read 2 Peter 3:11,17-18 in the margin. How should believers respond to their suffering as they await God's justice?
☐ **Retaliate in kind.** ☐ **Live holy lives.** ☐ **Grow in Christ.**
☐ **Beware of false teachings.** ☐ **Compromise their beliefs.**

Peter was convinced that although Christ had not returned as soon as some expected, He would return. Until then Christians should be wary of false teachers and continue to "grow in the grace and knowledge of our Lord and Savior Jesus Christ" (2 Pet. 3:18).

Suffering in the Books of 1–3 John
John's letters make two significant contributions to our understanding of evil and suffering.

Suffering cannot be attributed to the physical world. John wrote: "Do not love the world or the things that belong to the world. If anyone loves the world, love for the Father is not in him. Because everything that belongs to the world—the lust of the flesh, the lust of the eyes, and the pride in one's lifestyle—is not from the Father, but is from the world" (1 John 2:15-16). When John told us not to love the world, he was not referring to God's physical creation but to things of the evil world system that seek to draw us away from a holy lifestyle—sin, selfishness, and evil desires. In fact, many scholars suggest that John's letters, like his Gospel, were partly written to refute the challenge of Gnosticism. The Gnostics were dualists, people who believed that the physical world is inherently evil. They considered the spiritual realm totally distinct from the physical world. Because of their dualism, Gnostics could not accept Jesus' humanity. The Gnostics were Docetics. Docetism is the belief that Jesus seemed to be human but was not really a man.

18. Read these verses and state how they refute Docetism.

1 John 4:3: _____

John 1:14: _____

John identified Docetism with the spirit of the antichrist and focused on Jesus' incarnation. God's Son came to earth as a man.

"Since all these things are to be destroyed in this way, it is clear what sort of people you should be in holy conduct and godliness. Since you have been forwarned, be on your guard, so that you are not led away by the error of the immoral and fall from your own stability. But grow in the grace and knowledge of our Lord and Savior Jesus Christ."
2 Peter 3:11,17-18

Gnosticism
The belief that the physical world is evil

Docetism
The belief that Jesus only seemed to be human

"Every spirit who does not confess Jesus is not from God. This is the spirit of the antichrist."
1 John 4:3

"The Word became flesh and took up residence among us."
John 1:14

Fear No Evil

John's rejection of Docetism and Gnostic dualism reminds us that the Bible never tries to explain our suffering merely as the result of being finite or physical. To some Greeks, finitude or limitation meant imperfection or evil; therefore, the only way to escape suffering was to escape this physical world. Although John urged us not to love the world, he was not proposing an escapist attitude.

19. Check the correct emphasis in John's teachings.
☐ **Blame your suffering on the physical world.**
☐ **Reject fleshly desires that interfere with holy living.**

God's love drives out fear and ensures victory. John also stressed God's love as a response to evil and suffering. Although John did not promise exemption from evil because of God's love, he echoed a note of victory similar to that of Jesus: "'You will have suffering in this world. Be courageous! I have conquered the world'" (John 16:33). A Christian who knows God's love and grows in loving relationships with others, John taught, should have no fear: "There is no fear in love; instead, perfect love drives out fear, because fear involves punishment. So the one who fears has not reached perfection in love" (1 John 4:18). John applied this teaching to two potential objects of fear: the world and God.

- Early Christians who knew of the world's opposition to them were likely fearful. John wrote, "Do not be surprised, brothers, if the world hates you" (1 John 3:13).

"You are from God, little children, and you have conquered them, because the One who is in you is greater than the one who is in the world."
1 John 4:4

20. Read 1 John 4:4. Circle a believer's source of security.

John's encouragement lay in the fact that whoever abides in God is secure and confident. Believers are on the victorious side of the struggle between good and evil. Because of our faith we can overcome the world: "Whatever has been born of God conquers the world. This is the victory that has conquered the world: our faith" (1 John 5:4). John was not suggesting that believing harder will automatically ease our problems, for our faith is rooted in God's power over the world. Our faith is in God, not in our faith. Therefore, Christians should not be paranoid about the world or its power. The Devil is not equal to Christ (see 1 John 3:8).

• John knew that Christians might also fear God's judgment. But he explained that Christians need have no fear if they remain in God and obey Him. Although John did not expect sinless perfection (see 1 John 1:8-10), he encouraged clear loyalty to God (see 1 John 2:3-6). Remaining in God would help Christians "not be ashamed before Him at His coming" (1 John 2:28).

21. Read 1 John 4:17-18. Why do people fear God's judgment?
_____

What is the antidote to fear? _____

Fear of God is due to a fear of punishment for sin, but "perfect love drives out fear" (1 John 4:18). The Christian life is one of joy, not fear (see 1 John 1:4; 2 John 12). Christians have confidence before God because He is willing to forgive sins (see 1 John 3:21-22), and He lovingly gave us commandments as guides to help us avoid unnecessary hardship (see 1 John 5:3).

22. Stop and pray about any fears you have. Claim Christ's victory over the world and His love that conquers all fear.

Suffering in the Book of Revelation

Revelation, an apocalyptic book, was written by John while he was in exile because of his faith (see Rev. 1:9). Although a lot of people study Revelation primarily to learn about the future, the original readers were largely concerned with its insight into suffering. John was writing in the late first century, when the persecution of Christians was direct and widespread. The Book of Revelation offers a perspective on suffering that speaks to believers today, since we live in a time when opposition against us is rapidly growing.

God is ultimately in control of history. John assured suffering Christians that although the forces of evil might seem victorious for a while, God's victory will eventually be obvious:

> *The kingdom of the world has become the kingdom*
> *of our Lord and of His Messiah,*
> *and He will reign forever and ever.* Revelation 11:15

"Love is perfected with us so that we may have confidence in the day of judgment; for we are as He is in this world. There is no fear in love; instead, perfect love drives out fear, because fear involves punishment. So the one who fears has not reached perfection in love." 1 John 4:17-18

Apocalyptic
Revealing or unveiling. Apocalyptic literature like Daniel and Revelation reflects the persecution of God's people and predicts a future judgment that brings punishment for the wicked and rewards for the faithful.

John was confident that God rules the universe: "'I am the Alpha and the Omega,' says the Lord God, 'the One who is, who was, and who is coming, the Almighty'" (Rev. 1:8).

23. Do you believe that God is in control of all things?
☐ Yes ☐ No   How does your belief affect your understanding of the presence of evil and suffering in the world today?
☐ It helps me trust God in all circumstances.
☐ It causes me to question why suffering and evil exist.
☐ It strengthens my resolve to be faithful in suffering.

God is just and will judge the wicked. Much of the Book of Revelation is devoted to God's punishment of the wicked. The martyrs John saw in heaven asked the question that many of John's readers probably posed: "'O Lord, holy and true, how long until You judge and avenge our blood from those who live on the earth?'" (Rev. 6:10). The seven seals, the seven trumpets, and the seven bowls all reveal God's answer. The letters to the seven churches also point to God's concern to reward the faithful and to punish the faithless.

24. What do you believe about God's justice?
☐ God is just all the time.
☐ God's justice is perfect, and I can trust His timing.
☐ God's justice is perfect, so I don't have to take vengeance.
☐ I see no evidence of God's justice, so I don't believe it exists.

God will eventually transform the world, eliminating all evil and suffering. Even though the original readers of Revelation knew they might continue to suffer persecution and perhaps even die for their faith, they were encouraged by John's assurance that suffering would end in the future.

"[God] will wipe away every tear from their eyes.
Death will exist no longer;
grief, crying, and pain will exist no longer, because the previous things have passed away."
Revelation 21:4

25. Read Revelation 21:4 in the margin. Which form of suffering do you most long to see relieved?
☐ Physical death   ☐ Grief   ☐ Sorrow   ☐ Pain
☐ Injustice   ☐ Cruelty   ☐ Abuse   ☐ Illness

One day God will remove suffering from the world and will dwell among His people (see Rev. 21:3,22).

Jesus is the coming Victor and Lord. Jesus appears in Revelation primarily as a military victor who battles and destroys the forces of evil (see Rev. 19:11-16). To the original audience, impressed by the strength of the Roman Empire, this reminder of Christ's power would have been reassuring. Christ has "'the keys of Death and Hades'" (Rev. 1:18). Our glorious King will return one day and set everything right. No power is greater than His.

Christians are called to endure. John identified endurance as the basic perspective of faithful, persecuted Christians. He explained that believers shared "the tribulation, kingdom, and perseverance in Jesus" (Rev. 1:9). He also expressed Christ's compliments to the churches in Ephesus, Thyatira, and Philadelphia for their endurance (see Rev. 2:2-3,19; 3:10). Revelation teaches that courage is both needed and commendable in the face of persecution.

> *"'I know your works, your labor, and your endurance, and that you cannot tolerate evil. You have tested those who call themselves apostles and are not, and you have found them to be liars. You also possess endurance and have tolerated many things because of My name, and have not grown weary.'"*
> Revelation 2:2-3

While patient endurance is the major virtue in Revelation, cowardice is the major vice (see Rev. 21:8). The context of persecution required a decisive commitment to the Christian faith. Believers could either courageously proclaim Jesus or hold their silence in cowardice. Jesus probably had this kind of situation in mind when He reversed the pattern of retribution. Jesus called His disciples blessed when they are persecuted and pronounced a warning on us "when all people speak well" of us (Luke 6:26). The traditional doctrine of retribution could be diagrammed like this:

Bad ➜ suffering   Good ➜ success

In a time of persecution, however, the formula is changed:

Courage ➜ suffering   Cowardice ➜ success

26. How do you see courage leading to suffering today? _____

_____

How do you see cowardice leading to success? _____

_____

John, like Jesus, knew that faithfulness would lead to suffering, but that prospect could not become an excuse for believers to hide or neglect their commitment to God. Nor should we adopt the values and ways of the pagan society to avoid suffering (see Rev. 18:4).

John's advice to his readers is amazingly relevant to us. Christians around the world face persecution by hostile governments, and someday believers in America may face this threat.

27. In some ways our government discourages the expression of Christian faith. ☐ Agree ☐ Disagree   **Government opposition to Christianity is increasing.** ☐ Agree ☐ Disagree

Throughout history believers have endured persecution for the cause of Christ. Many have given their lives for their faith.

The Book of Revelation does not promise immediate relief from suffering, but it assures believers that God will have the ultimate victory and that He will make everything new (see Rev. 21:5). In the meantime, believers are to boldly hold to their faith, knowing that God will empower them to persevere with hope in Jesus.

28. Review by completing the statements.
a. God is ultimately in control of _____.
b. God is _____ **and will judge the** _____.
c. God will eventually _____ **the world, eliminating**
   all _____ **and** _____.
d. Jesus is the coming _____ **and** _____.
e. Christians are called to _____.

Complete this self-assessment by checking all that apply.
☐ My openness about my faith makes me vulnerable to suffering.
☐ I am willing to suffer patiently in order to be in God's will.
☐ I do not compromise my faith to avoid suffering.
☐ I am confident that Jesus will return and end all suffering.

When You Suffer
Our study of the biblical views of evil and suffering has reminded us that God is concerned about suffering and that the Bible provides help to those who suffer. Let's review the biblical lessons we have learned and identify ways we can help alleviate human suffering.

"Come out of her,
My people,
so that you will not
share in her sins,
or receive any of
her plagues."
Revelation 18:4

Learning from Suffering

As we have seen, the biblical writers did not give simplistic answers to why we suffer. Instead, they dealt with practical understandings of how we can respond to suffering. Let's summarize these.

God is ultimately responsible for human suffering. As Creator, God is ultimately responsible for the world. He is sovereign. However, the Bible does not say that God directly causes all suffering. Although some proof texts seem to support divine determinism (see Ex. 4:11; Isa. 45:7; Amos 3:6), the biblical writers acknowledge the role that human freedom plays in causing pain and tragedy.

God is ultimately responsible for human suffering.

29. Think about suffering you are experiencing and check the statement you most closely agree with. God—
☐ **caused it;** ☐ **allowed it;** ☐ **had nothing to do with it.**

God is ultimately responsible for human suffering because He either causes it to happen or allows it to happen. For example, God did not cause your car wreck, but He created a world in which accidents can happen. Although God created a world with the possibility of suffering, He does not directly cause all pain.

Sin causes some human suffering. The Bible repeatedly stresses that actions have consequences. The doctrine of retribution is the belief that if you are good, you will prosper; if you are bad, you will suffer. As a general rule of thumb, this concept seems fair. A moral God who governs our universe and allows human freedom is just in rewarding and punishing us in this way.

As we have seen, however, several biblical figures warn us not to strictly apply the retributive principle to every instance of suffering. Retribution is not a totally comprehensive, foolproof explanation of all hardship. Although sin leads to suffering, it is not the only cause. Perhaps someone else's sin causes our pain. Therefore, we should not try to judge someone else's faith or lack of faith by the amount of suffering they experience.

Suffering can produce greater self-understanding. The experience of suffering has been described as a "vale of soul-making" because sometimes we emerge from that experience with a more honest, realistic view of ourselves.[3] Job's experience, for example, prompted serious self-examination (see Job 31). Many biblical writers stress that suffering can be a learning experience, producing greater self-understanding. However, the Bible also acknowledges that some people may never benefit from their suffering.

30. Identify something suffering has taught you about yourself.

_____

Suffering can develop deeper faith in God. Frequently individuals emerge from suffering with a better understanding of God (see Gen. 45:7). C. S. Lewis once described pain as God's megaphone.[4] God may not cause our suffering to get our attention, but He can use our crises to remind us of His claim on our lives.

This doesn't mean we should turn to God only in times of trouble. Nor should we assume we can have a total understanding of God, ourselves, and our suffering in this life. We may know some of the reasons for our suffering, but an element of mystery always remains in our earthly existence.

"We know in part, and we prophesy in part. But when the perfect comes, the partial will come to an end. When I was a child, I spoke like a child, I thought like a child, I reasoned like a child. When I became a man, I put aside childish things. For now we see indistinctly, as in a mirror, but then face to face. Now I know in part, but then I will know fully, as I am fully known."
1 Corinthians 13:9-12

31. Read 1 Corinthians 13:9-12 in the margin. Identify uncertainties you are willing to relinquish and assurances you will embrace. Check the appropriate column for each statement.

	I WILL RELINQUISH	I WILL EMBRACE
Fear of the unknown	☐	☐
Fear of evil	☐	☐
The need to know why suffering exists	☐	☐
Doubt about God's justice in the world	☐	☐
Hope in eternity with Christ	☐	☐
Knowledge that God is in control	☐	☐
Understanding that God wants good for you	☐	☐
Questioning God about His decisions	☐	☐
Assurance that you are God's child	☐	☐

Innocent suffering can be part of the redemptive process. No one deserved suffering less than Jesus, whose innocent suffering was essential to our salvation (see 1 Pet. 2:24). The redemptive role of His ordeal suggests that suffering can be used to serve others. Innocent human suffering cannot save ourselves or others, but it can sacrificially serve those around us and can have a redemptive function. Christians who boldly and faithfully respond to persecution can influence non-Christian observers.

God responds to our suffering with compassion and comfort. When we suffer, God is aware of our condition and empathizes with us. " 'I am compassionate,' " God told the Hebrews (Ex. 22:27). God strengthens and encourages us in our suffering. He occasionally removes our suffering miraculously, but He often provides companionship and strength while the problem remains. When we walk through the valley of suffering, we can "fear no evil" because He is with us (Ps. 23:4, NIV).

God works for good in all situations. Paul reminds us that "in all things God works for the good of those who love him, who have been called according to his purpose" (Rom. 8:28, NIV). Paul did not say that everything that happens to us is good but that God works for good in everything. God's omnicompetence is God's ability to bring good from all situations. There is no situation beyond God's love and power. God is good, and He wills good for us. When we face "the fiery ordeal" of suffering (1 Pet. 4:12), we can "cast all [our] anxiety on him because he cares for [us]" (1 Pet. 5:7, NIV).

God works for good in all situations.

32. How effectively do you cast all your cares on God?
☐ **I find it difficult to trust that He works for good in my suffering.**
☐ **I ultimately trust Him but still worry.**
☐ **I completely turn over my suffering to Him.**

Responding to Evil and Suffering

How should Christians respond to the presence of evil in the world, and how can we help those who suffer? As "God's co-workers" (1 Cor. 3:9), believers have specific responsibilities for overcoming evil and for responding to the suffering around us.

Fight evil. The Apostle Paul encouraged Christians in Rome to fight evil: "Detest evil; cling to what is good" (Rom. 12:9). Believers are to fight evil by following biblical ethical principles: "Do not be conquered by evil, but conquer evil with good" (Rom. 12:21). Christians can fight evil in several ways.

- We can resist Satan and the temptation to sin (see 1 Pet. 5:8-9).
- We can recognize and expose the prevalence of evil in our society (see Eph. 5:11).
- We can work for the causes of truth, justice, and freedom in our society. Jesus described His followers as salt and light (see Matt. 5:13-16). When we faithfully live for Christ and share the message of salvation in Him, we can have a redemptive influence on the world around us. Christians are called to be change agents, and the only way to change evil is through the transforming power of Jesus Christ.

33. What social evils and injustices require believers' immediate attention and action?

_____   _____   _____

Circle the need that you feel is most pressing.

What will you do to address the need? _____

_____

- We can combine prayer and political activism. We can pray for God's help to resist evil in our lives and to overcome evil in society, vote our Christian consciences, volunteer in humanitarian organizations, choose careers that oppose injustice, inform others about the evil we see in our world, and share the good news of Jesus Christ. By doing these things, we do our part to usher in God's kingdom on earth.

34. Name three issues or persons you will begin praying for as a result of this study.

_____   _____   _____

Be concerned about those suffering around you. The misery of others should concern believers. Jesus taught, "Be compassionate as your Father is compassionate" (Luke 6:36, NEB). We should "put on heartfelt compassion" (Col. 3:12) for those who hurt.

"Be sober! Be on the alert! Your adversary the Devil is prowling around like a roaring lion, looking for anyone he can devour. Resist him, firm in the faith, knowing that the same sufferings are being experienced by your brothers in the world."
1 Peter 5:8-9

"Don't participate in the fruitless works of darkness, but instead, expose them."
Ephesians 5:11

Our concern for others should be comprehensive. We should be alert to the needs of individuals and groups—an individual with a terminal disease as well as religious or ethnic groups that are targeted for extermination. We should be just as concerned about a sufferer in China as one on the next block. We should be as concerned about emotional, psychological, and spiritual suffering as about physical illness. Loneliness, despair, and alienation are frequently just as painful as disease.

35. Identify an example of each form of suffering in your community.
Physical: _____
Emotional: _____
Psychological: _____
Spiritual: _____

Be actively involved in alleviating suffering. Debbie Alexander went to her church in Weddington, North Carolina, to hear a boys choir from Liberia that was touring the United States to raise money for their orphanage. The boys' parents and many of their other family members had been slaughtered in a civil war that had ravaged their country. God spoke to Debbie during that concert, and she and her husband decided to adopt two of the boys, David and Seeboe. The next year God led them to adopt David's sisters, Mercy and Teta; his brother, James; and Seeboe's "blood brother," Joe.

Knowing about suffering is not enough. Although not everyone is called to do what Debbie and her husband did, we should actively respond to the suffering we observe. Our help might take many forms. We often respond to crises such as the death of a friend or a drought in Ethiopia, but we could also work to prevent suffering. Our actions can be personal and private, such as sitting with a sick friend in a hospital room, or they can be public and political, such as writing to our representative in Congress about proposed legislation. Our concern for the suffering does not need to be restricted to religious or spiritual activities. Jesus was concerned about the total person, and he did not separate the spiritual from the secular.

Although Jesus recognized that " 'you always have the poor with you' " (John 12:8), He did not stop helping them. We cannot eliminate all suffering, and some of the suffering we address cannot be

Knowing about suffering is not enough.

When we suffer,
our ultimate resource
is the God who cares
for us.

eliminated in this life. We must rely on God's strength and wisdom in order to make a difference. Therefore, a Christian's most valuable resource is prayer. Our concern for the suffering can express itself through prayer and social programs, piety and politics. When we suffer, our ultimate resource is the God who cares for us.

How should we respond to suffering? By imitating the God who identifies with our suffering and helps us through our trials. We can make the hymn writer's words our prayer:

Enable us to hear the cries
Of those who, in despair,
Call out for someone who will hear,
For someone who will care.
Then, hearing, let us actively
Pursue with one accord
A ministry which meets their needs:
Give us thy love, O Lord.[5]

36. Which steps will you take to fight evil and alleviate suffering?
☐ **I will pray about my involvement.**
☐ **I will research needs and solutions.**
☐ **I will participate in ministry.**
☐ **I will counsel those who hurt.**
☐ **I will seek political or social redress.**
☐ **Other:** _____
_____
_____

[1] "The Martyrdom of Polycarp, Bishop of Smyrna, as Told in the Letter of the Church of Smyrna to the Church of Philomelium," in *Early Christian Fathers*, trans. and ed. Cyril C. Richardson (New York: Simon and Schuster, 1996), 152.
[2] David C. Gibbs Jr., "The Legal Implications of Witnessing at Work," *Christianity Today* [online], 29 October 2004 [cited 7 July 2005]. Available from the Internet: *www.christianitytoday.com/workplace/articles/legalimplications.html*.
[3] John Hick, *Evil and the God of Love* (London: Collins, 1968), 289–97.
[4] C. S. Lewis, *The Problem of Pain* (New York: Macmillan, 1962), 92.
[5] "O Lord, Who Came to Earth to Show," *Baptist Hymnal* (Nashville: Convention Press, 1975), no. 309.

Leader Guide

Fear No Evil explores the biblical views of evil and suffering. After this study, participants will be able to—

- identify causes of evil and suffering;
- explain God's role when they suffer;
- name types and sources of suffering;
- explain how God intervenes in the lives of people who suffer;
- cite examples of suffering in the Bible;
- explain why Christ is the only answer to the problem of sin;
- describe a Christian response to evil and suffering;
- cite Scripture passages that offer hope in suffering;
- help people who suffer.

This leader guide will help you facilitate six group sessions of 1 to 1½ hours each. Each session of this leader guide provides the following segments that equip you to prepare for and lead the study:

- "Prepare" lists materials to gather and teaching tools to prepare in advance.
- "Probe" examines key Scripture passages and concepts in the chapter.
- "Personalize" helps members internalize truths and apply them to life.

Session 1

After the session members will be able to—

- define *sin*, *suffering*, and *evil*;
- identify common questions about evil and suffering;
- identify characteristics of moral suffering and natural suffering;
- describe retribution as a source of suffering;

- distinguish between God's omnipotence and humans' free will.

Prepare

1. Read the entire book to understand the scope and topics of study. Study chapter 1 in depth and complete the learning activities. Examine the learning goals for the study and for this session.

2. Distribute copies of *Fear No Evil* in advance. Ask participants to read chapter 1 and to complete the learning activities before session 1.

3. Watch newspapers and magazines for articles that demonstrate evil and suffering. Clip and post these on the wall at the front of the room.

4. Record the following title and questions on a tear sheet.

   Guiding Questions for Our Study
   - *Why do evil and suffering exist?*
   - *What is God's role in evil and suffering?*
   - *What does the Bible say about evil and suffering?*
   - *How should a Christian respond to evil and suffering?*
   - *What biblical examples offer us hope, encouragement, and instruction?*

5. Prepare tear sheets with the following definitions.
   - *Sin: Using our freedom of choice to rebel against God*
   - *Evil: People, powers, influences, and actions that oppose God and His purposes*
   - *Suffering: The deeply personal response to a catastrophic or devastating event that brings overwhelming turmoil to our physical, emotional, or spiritual well-being*

6. Draw the following diagram in larger dimensions on a tear sheet.

Types of Suffering

7. Enlist two members to explain the two contexts for the study. Direct them to pages 12–14 in chapter 1.
8. Make three placards with one of these statements on each:
   * *When we suffer, God is all-powerful.*
   * *When we suffer, God cares.*
   * *When we suffer, God helps.*
9. Have tear sheets and markers available.

Probe

1. Introduce the general topic of this study. Point to the news items on the wall and highlight the pervasiveness of evil and suffering. Ask, What questions come to mind when you see suffering and tragedies? Display and read the tear sheet *Guiding Questions for Our Study* and explain that these questions will shape the study. Keep them posted throughout the study.
2. Ask members to turn to "How Do You See It?" on page 155 and to record their answers in the session 1 column. State that members will use the same survey in session 6 to evaluate their learning.

3. Divide members into three groups and give each group a tear sheet and a marker. Ask one group to define *sin,* another *evil,* and the third *suffering.* Have the groups record their definitions and share them with the large group. Display the tear sheets with the definitions you prepared in advance. Explain that these will be our working definitions for this study. Leave them on display throughout the study.
4. Ask, What two categories of suffering are named in chapter 1? (moral, natural) Review the definitions on pages 9 and 11. Display the tear sheet *Types of Suffering.* Ask members to name characteristics of moral and natural suffering. List these in the circles on the tear sheet. Then ask them to name qualities shared by both types. List these in the area of the diagram that overlaps. (Possible responses: *Moral*—caused by sin, hard to understand. *Natural*—not caused by sin, more understandable. *Both*—cause pain, can have innocent victims.) Ask: To what extent do you think God is responsible for moral suffering? For natural suffering? To what extent do you think humans are responsible for moral suffering? For natural suffering?
5. Introduce the concept of retributive suffering and explain that this important theme will reappear throughout the study. Ask for responses to activity 4 on page 10. Ask: How does the principle of retribution cause suffering in the world today? Does the operation of this principle mean that God is responsible for suffering? Use the ideas on page 11 to guide the discussion.
6. Call on the members enlisted to explain the two contexts for our study.

7. Call on a member to read Daniel 3:13-18. State that this account introduces God's omnipotence, a key theme in our study. Ask a volunteer to define *omnipotence* (p. 16). Show the first placard: *When we suffer, God is all-powerful.* Divide members into two groups and ask each group to discuss and report on one of the misconceptions on pages 17–20.

8. Call on a member to read Daniel 3:17. Display the second placard: *When we suffer, God cares.* Ask a volunteer to distinguish between the terms *compassion* and *comfort* (p. 21). Ask members to share ways they have experienced God's compassion and His comfort.

9. Call on a member to read Daniel 3:18,25. Display the third placard: *When we suffer, God helps.* Review the misconceptions about the meaning of God's help on pages 24–27. Ask volunteers to share ways they have experienced God's help in suffering.

10. Conclude that the account in Daniel reinforces a proper understanding of God's relationship to suffering. When Shadrach, Meshach, and Abednego faced a fiery ordeal, God was in the furnace with them.

Personalize

1. Direct members to page 3 and overview the subjects of this study. Share the learning goals for the study on page 143.

2. Ask members to read chapter 2 and to complete the learning activities before the next session. Close with prayer.

Session 2

After the session members will be able to—

- describe the relationship of human sin to suffering;
- affirm God's sovereignty in the face of human suffering;
- identify ways suffering is punishment for sin;
- give evidence that God has compassion for those who suffer;
- identify ways they can show concern for suffering.

Prepare

1. Study chapter 2 and complete the learning activities.

2. Prepare a placard titled *The Consequence of Sin* = _____.

3. Enlist a member to explain Joseph's view of God's sovereignty and another member to report on the interplay between Pharaoh's free will and God's sovereignty. Both members should use the Scriptures and ideas in "Suffering and God's Sovereignty," pages 33–36.

4. Enlist a member to report on ways the Old Testament laws express caring for those who suffer. Direct the person to "Caring for Those Who Suffer," beginning on page 46.

Probe

1. Ask, What evidence of moral decline do you see in our culture? List responses on a tear sheet or dry-erase board. Ask, What are some ways society tries to fix some of these problems? (Legislation, law enforcement, citizen-action agencies, community-assistance agencies) Ask, What do these interventions fail to address? (Sin)

2. Refer to the definition of *sin* (posted on the wall from session 1) and to the placard *The Consequence of Sin* = _____. Say, We will turn to Scripture to fill in this blank. Direct members to Genesis 3. Review the fall of humanity in Genesis 3:1-7. Emphasize the bulleted summary points on page 32. Ask for responses to activity 5 on that page. Ask, What is the relationship of human sin to suffering? (Sin brought terrible consequences—our inherited sin nature, our alienation from God and other people, and the corruption of the natural world.) Ask, What is the ultimate consequence of sin? (Spiritual and physical death) Return to the placard and fill in the blank with the word *death*. Ask, What is the ultimate remedy for sin? (Jesus' sacrifice for sin)

3. Call on the two members enlisted to explain Joseph's view of God's sovereignty and to report on the interplay between Pharaoh's free will and God's sovereignty. Read Exodus 4:11 and ask: Is God the author of evil? (No) Were evil and suffering part of God's original plan? (No, they are perversions of His good creation.) What causes sickness, suffering, and pain in our world? (Our world is fallen because of humanity's choice to rebel against God.) Can God work through bad situations to bring about His good plan? (Yes, as seen in Joseph's story)

4. Ask, Can anyone recall the definition of the doctrine of retribution from session 1? Use the scriptural examples on pages 38–39 to show that the Pentateuch identifies the retributive principle as a cause of suffering. Divide members into three groups and assign each group to explain and give scriptural examples of the three aspects of retribution in the Pentateuch discussed on pages 40–41. After group work, call for reports. Summarize by pointing out that the retributive principle is consistent with the ideas of God's justice, human free will, and human responsibility. Remind members that retribution is only one biblical explanation of suffering.

5. Read Exodus 34:6-7. State, God has compassion for those who suffer. Refer to activity 17 on pages 42–43 and to the five ways God interacts with us in compassion, based on Exodus 3:7-8. Give other examples of God's compassion for suffering people, emphasizing that God hears our cry for help, gives us a second chance, and disciplines us. Ask for responses to activity 20 on page 45.

6. Explain that because God cares for those who suffer, He expect us to care as well. Call on the member enlisted to report on ways the Old Testament laws express caring for those who suffer. Ask: What ministries does our church have for suffering people? What else can we do? Call for responses to activity 23 on page 48.

Personalize

1. Direct members to "Lessons from the Pentateuch" on page 156. Ask them to write implications of each lesson they learned in their study of the Pentateuch.

2. Ask members to read chapter 3 and to complete the learning activities before the next session. Close with prayer.

Session 3

After the session members will be able to—
- describe God's use of retribution to discipline spiritually rebellious people;
- summarize God's view of innocent suffering;
- state the importance of individual responsibility for actions;
- explain why Jesus' suffering was redemptive;
- affirm the certainty of future deliverance from suffering;
- name ways God identifies with those who suffer;
- identify limits on the doctrine of retribution;
- affirm God's sovereignty in spite of human suffering.

Prepare

1. Study chapter 3 and complete the learning activities.
2. Draw the following diagram in larger dimensions on a tear sheet.

The Cycle of Sin and Repentance

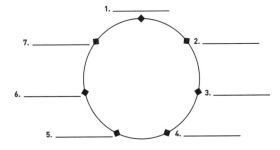

3. Enlist a member to summarize Jeremiah's and Ezekiel's teachings on individual accountability. Refer the person to "Individual Responsibility," pages 57–59.

4. Prepare a tear sheet with the stages in the development of the Hebrew view of suffering:
   Stage 1: All sufferers are sinners (retribution).
   Stage 2: Some sufferers are innocent.
   Stage 3: Some sufferers are saviors.
5. Enlist a member to illustrate how the psalms of lament question the doctrine of retribution. Refer the member to "Psalms of Suffering," pages 64–66.
6. Provide paper and pencils or pens.

Probe

1. Display the tear sheet *The Cycle of Sin and Repentance.* Use Judges 2:10-23 to present the Hebrews' cycle of repeated sin and God's interventions through His prophets. Fill in the steps as you guide a discussion of each stage of the cycle: (1) devotion, (2) compromise, (3) acts of disobedience (sin), (4) lifestyles of disobedience, (5) the prophet's call to repent, (6) God's discipline through oppression, (7) repentance. Point out God's use of retribution in this cycle. Ask, What was God's purpose in bringing discipline? (Repentance, return to God, restoration of relationship)
2. Call for responses to activities 2 and 3 on page 53. Refer again to the tear sheet *The Cycle of Sin and Repentance.* Ask, Where is America in this cycle?
3. State that not all suffering can be explained by the doctrine of retribution. Read Amos 5:12 and ask members to identify the three crimes of which the Hebrews were guilty. Use Jeremiah's teachings as summarized in "Innocent Suffering" on pages 56–57 to explain that some suffering is innocent,

the rich and powerful are held accountable for oppressing the poor, and God will
vindicate the poor.

4. Call on the member enlisted to summarize Jeremiah's and Ezekiel's teachings on
individual responsibility. Contrast this view
with the corporate accountability emphasized in the Pentateuch (see p. 58 or chap.
2, p. 40). State that the Hebrews were not
sent into exile because of their ancestors'
sins but because of their own sins. Ask:
What corporate or family sins can cause
suffering today? (Abuse, dysfunction,
societal wrongs) Does the existence of
corporate sin mean that individuals are not
accountable? (No, we are still acccount-
able to God for our sins.) What can individuals do to break these cycles of sin?

5. Display the tear sheet with the stages in
the development of the Hebrew view of
suffering. Identify the third stage as the
role of the Suffering Servant, Jesus Christ,
as articulated by Isaiah. Summarize God's
role in bringing Israel's suffering, comfort-
ing them, and redeeming them. State that
the Suffering Servant passages in Isaiah
also point to an individual who suffers on
behalf of the sinful. Ask a volunteer to
read Isaiah 53:4-5. Call for responses to
activity 12 on pages 60–61.

6. State that the prophets also responded to
unjust suffering by emphasizing God's
ultimate justice. Ask: What is an example of suffering today that awaits God's
vindication? How does the assurance of
ultimate justice help you deal with suffering and injustice?

7. Emphasize God's compassion for suffering
people in spite of their sin. Briefly mention the biblical examples in activity 18 on
page 63. Ask, How do we differ from God
in this respect? (We often don't feel compassion toward sinners.)

8. Call on the member enlisted to illustrate
how the psalms of lament question the
doctrine of retribution. Summarize that
these psalms express confidence in God's
ultimate justice and assure us of His presence through our suffering.

9. Divide members into three groups and
assign each group one of the following sections in chapter 3: "Wisdom in Suffering,"
(p. 66), "Learning Through Suffering"
(p. 68), and "Questions from Suffering"
(p. 71). Ask each group to review the
assigned topic and to summarize how the
biblical book addresses the doctrine of
retribution. As groups report, point out
ways these teachings differ from previous
treatments of the theme of retribution.

10. Use the story of Esther to affirm God's
providence in the face of great evil. Draw
a parallel between the Jews' self-defense
and believers' modern efforts to address
social problems. Call for responses to
activity 30 on page 73.

Personalize

1. Ask volunteers to state what they learned in
this session that helps them respond to the
following realities about suffering: Some suffering is undeserved. Sometimes the wicked
prosper. Payment for sin may be delayed.
The cause of some suffering is mysterious.

2. Ask members to read chapter 4 and to
complete the learning activities before the
next session. Close with prayer.

Session 4

After the session members will be able to—
- identify ways Jesus relieves suffering;
- explain why following Jesus can bring suffering;
- identify ways Jesus showed compassion for the suffering;
- respond to Christ's call for believers to minister to those who suffer;
- summarize Jesus' teachings on suffering;
- state the purpose of Jesus' suffering;
- describe how the Holy Spirit helps believers who suffer.

Prepare

1. Study chapter 4 and complete the learning activities.
2. Prepare the following placards.
   - *Jesus offered relief from legalism.*
   - *Jesus offered God's love.*
   - *Jesus offered accessibility to God.*
   - *Jesus offered a relationship with God.*
3. Enlist a member to report on ways Jesus' teachings on suffering affirmed the doctrine of retribution and another member to report on ways Jesus' teachings on suffering denied the doctrine of retribution. Refer the members to the section "Jesus Taught on Suffering," pages 85–89.
4. Write the heading *What Jesus' Suffering Teaches Us* at the top of a tear sheet. Make two columns with the following statements in the left column.
   - *Jesus did not retaliate against His accusers.*
   - *Jesus' attitude toward His death represents Scripture's paradoxical view.*
   - *Jesus' death was the ultimate revelation of God's identification with His people.*

Probe

1. Divide members into four groups and give each group one of the placards you prepared. Ask each group to review the corresponding section in chapter 4 (pp. 76–78) and to summarize the assigned way Jesus relieved suffering. Allow time for groups to work. Then call for reports.
2. Read Luke 9:23 and ask for responses to activity 5 on page 79. Emphasize the suffering of early believers. Ask, How do believers suffer for the gospel today?
3. Have volunteers read the passages in the margin on page 80. Ask, What was Jesus' motivation for helping these people? Stress Jesus' understanding of His ministry as expressed in Luke 4:18-19. Ask members to scan the section "Jesus Showed Compassion for the Suffering" (p. 80), to identify the four types of miracles Jesus performed to relieve suffering, and to give an example of each. Call for responses to activity 10 on page 82. State that whether or not Jesus healed physically, His goal for the person was spiritual wholeness and abundant life through a relationship with Himself.
4. State that Jesus taught His followers to have compassion for suffering as He did. Summarize Jesus' teaching in Matthew 25:31-46 and state that by relieving suffering, believers share Jesus' compassion and love with others. Ask a volunteer to explain the difference between a ministry and a humanitarian effort. Say, We are called to share Christ as the answer to all needs.
5. Call on the two members enlisted to report on ways Jesus' teachings on suffering affirmed and denied the doctrine of

retribution. Make sure the reporters mention key scriptural examples given in "Jesus Taught on Suffering." Ask, Was Jesus being inconsistent? (No, He affirmed that retribution operates as part of the moral order of things, but it cannot be used to explain all suffering. Everyone suffers because of our world's fallen nature.) Lead members to discuss activity 23 on page 89.

6. State that Jesus' suffering and death were intentional components of God's redemptive plan. Ask volunteers to read Acts 8:32-33 and 1 Peter 3:18. Ask for responses to activity 25 on page 90. Display the tear sheet *What Jesus' Suffering Teaches Us*. Discuss each point in the left column, using the Scriptures and ideas on pages 91–93. Ask members to explain what we learn from Jesus' example. List responses in the righthand column on the tear sheet.

7. State that we can rely on the Holy Spirit's presence and power when we suffer. Read John 14:16-18. Explain the identity of the Holy Spirit as Comforter. (He strengthens and encourages us in our suffering.) Mention His role in helping the early Christians face persecution.

Personalize

1. Ask members to complete "What's Your Fear/Faith Factor?" on page 157 and to calculate their totals. Remind members that Jesus and the Holy Spirit are with us when we suffer and face evil.

2. Read 2 Corinthians 1:3-5. Challenge members to comfort those who are suffering and to offer Jesus as their hope.

3. Ask members to read chapter 5 and to complete the learning activities before the next session. Close with prayer.

Session 5

After the session members will be able to—
- name ways Paul suffered for Christ;
- describe the consequences of sin;
- identify the solution to the suffering caused by sin;
- list arenas in which believers suffer for the gospel;
- state what it means to share in Christ's suffering;
- assess their willingness to suffer for Christ;
- describe how believers can be prepared for spiritual warfare;
- identify three ways believers can respond to suffering.

Prepare

1. Study chapter 5 and complete the learning activities.

2. Prepare a tear sheet titled *Paul's Teachings on Suffering* with these points:
   - *Suffering Because of Sin*
   - *Suffering for the Gospel*
   - *Death and Suffering*
   - *Suffering from Demonic Attack*
   - *Responding to Suffering*

3. Draw this diagram on a tear sheet.

God's Wrath

4. Prepare placards with these statements:
   - *Sin merits God's wrath.*
   - *Sin leads to suffering.*
   - *We reap what we sow.*
   - *Satan deceives and destroys.*
   - *Christ saves us from the suffering caused by sin.*
5. Enlist a member to summarize Paul's view of death and the believer's hope in the face of death. Direct the member to "Death and Suffering," beginning on page 112.
6. Prepare a tear sheet titled *The Spiritual Armor* with two columns labeled *Armor* and *Function*. In the left column list the pieces of armor from Ephesians 6:14-17— belt of truth, breastplate of righteousness, sandals of peace, shield of faith, helmet of salvation, and sword of the Spirit.

Probe

1. Say, Countless Christians around the world suffer daily for following Christ. Direct members to "Profiles of Persecution" on page 158. Divide participants into two groups and assign each group one of the profiles. Instruct each group to read the profile and to discuss the questions at the top of the page.
2. Read 2 Corinthians 11:23-27 and state that these are ways Paul suffered during his ministry. Ask: Why did Paul endure this treatment? What motivated him to persevere in spite of intense suffering? Ask a member to read Acts 20:22-24. Ask: To what length was Paul willing to go for the gospel? (Death) Why did the churches' sin make Paul suffer? (Damaged the cause of Christ) How would our world be different if all believers shared Paul's sorrow for the

lost? Ask a member to read 2 Corinthians 12:7-10. Ask, What did Paul learn through physical suffering? Ask volunteers to name the four ways Paul suffered (pp. 98–102). Write these on a dry-erase board. Ask: Do believers today suffer in these ways for the cause of Christ? How?

3. Display the tear sheet *Paul's Teachings on Suffering*. Say, Paul's letters include a wealth of teachings on suffering. Point to *Suffering Because of Sin* and display the placard *Sin merits God's wrath*. Use Romans 1:18-25 to emphasize that all people are sinful by nature and deserve God's wrath. Show the process by which God turns sinners over to the consequences of their choices. Display the placards *Sin leads to suffering* and *We reap what we sow*. Ask, What are the consequences of sin? (Degradation, death, punishment) Summarize Paul's use of the doctrine of retribution, emphasizing that he stressed the eternal consequences of sin more than a cause-effect relationship between sin and suffering in this life. Display the placard *Satan deceives and destroys*. Give biblical examples of Satan's destructive influence, as well as God's use of Satan to test believers' faith or to bring God's punishment (pp. 105–6). Display the tear sheet *God's Wrath*. Ask members to interpret its meaning. (Without Christ a person is unprotected from God's wrath and must receive the penalty for his sin— death. A believer is sheltered from God's wrath because Christ has paid the penalty for our sin by dying on the cross.) Display and read the placard *Christ saves us from the suffering caused by sin.*

4. Point to *Suffering for the Gospel* on the tear sheet *Paul's Teachings on Suffering*. Divide members into three groups. Assign each group to review one of the subtopics in "Suffering for the Gospel" on pages 107–12 and to report on ways first-century believers could suffer at home, because of the state, or in the church. As the group reports on the home, ask, How can believers today have redemptive relationships with unsaved family members? As the group reports on the state, ask: How do believers in other countries suffer for Christ at the hands of the government? Do you think American believers will be persecuted by the government in the future? Use activity 16 on page 109 to discuss ways to express faith in an ungodly society. As the group reports on the church, ask, How can we apply Paul's teachings to relationships in churches today? Read Romans 8:16-18 and Colossians 1:24 and ask: What does it mean to share in Christ's suffering? How can believers share in Christ's suffering?

5. Point to *Death and Suffering* on the tear sheet *Paul's Teachings on Suffering*. Call on the member enlisted to summarize Paul's view of death and the believer's hope in the face of death.

6. Point to *Suffering from Demonic Attack* on the tear sheet *Paul's Teachings on Suffering*. Say, Although Satan and his demons have been defeated, they continue to fight. Ask for responses to activity 26 on page 115. Point out that believers must be prepared for spiritual battle. Ask a member to read Ephesians 6:14-17. Display the tear sheet *The Spiritual Armor* and ask members to state the way each piece of armor protects believers and equips us to wage war. Write responses in the righthand column.

7. Point to *Responding to Suffering* on the tear sheet *Paul's Teachings on Suffering* and state that Paul gave us practical ways to exercise faith when we suffer. Ask a member to read 2 Thessalonians 2:16-17. Write on a dry-erase board, *Place your hope in God*. Ask a member to read 2 Corinthians 1:3-4. Write on the dry-erase board, *Look to God for comfort*. Ask a member to read Romans 8:35-39. Write on the board, *Believe that God works for your good*. Point to the three principles on the board and ask, How can believers look to God in these ways when they suffer? Record responses on the board. Challenge members to depend on God in pain and trials.

Personalize

1. Ask, Are you willing to suffer for the gospel? Challenge members to pray about their commitment, as well as for persecuted believers throughout the world.

2. Ask members to read chapter 6 and to complete the learning activities before the next session. Close with prayer.

Session 6

After the session members will be able to—
- describe the role of faith in responding to suffering;
- affirm God's presence and power in suffering;
- identify purposes of God's testing;
- explain the role of patience in suffering;

- name ways believers suffer for Christ;
- explain how God will bring justice and eliminate evil and suffering;
- identify actions they will take to fight evil and alleviate suffering.

Prepare

1. Study chapter 6 and complete the learning activities.
2. Prepare a tear sheet with the following.
   - *Recognize the source of your suffering.*
   - *Be patient when you suffer.*
   - *Practice an active faith.*
   - *Don't be judgmental.*
   - *Don't complain.*
   - *Pray about your suffering.*
3. Enlist two members to summarize the two subtopics in "Suffering in the Books of 1–2 Peter" on pages 128–31.
4. Write these statements at the tops of separate tear sheets:
   - *God is ultimately in control of history.*
   - *God is just and will judge the wicked.*
   - *God will eventually transform the world, eliminating all evil and suffering.*
   - *Jesus is the coming Victor and Lord.*
   - *Christians are called to endure.*
5. Prepare the following placards.
   - *God is ultimately responsible for human suffering.*
   - *Sin causes some human suffering.*
   - *Suffering can produce greater self-understanding.*
   - *Suffering can develop deeper faith in God.*
   - *Innocent suffering can be part of the redemptive process.*
   - *God responds to our suffering with compassion and comfort.*
   - *God works for good in all situations.*
6. Enlist a member to report on ways believers can fight evil, using the material on pages 139–40 in chapter 6.
7. Have five markers for group work.

Probe

1. Read Hebrews 12:1-2. State that this session will identify guidelines from the general letters and Revelation for remaining faithful to Christ and for patiently enduring suffering for the gospel. Explain that these books were written against a backdrop of Christian persecution by the Roman Empire.
2. State that the writer of Hebrews emphasized the necessity of spiritual maturity when being persecuted for Christ. Ask, Why is spiritual maturity critical when facing suffering? Refer to the roll call of faith in Hebrews 11 and emphasize the importance of faith in facing suffering. Ask members to identify the proper object of faith. (Jesus) Ask volunteers to read Hebrews 2:14-15; 4:15-16. Ask, In what two ways is Jesus qualified to empower us when we suffer? (He was tested and suffered. He has defeated the Devil and death.) Ask a member to read Hebrews 12:5-11. Ask: What is the motivation behind God's discipline? What is the purpose of His discipline? Read Hebrews 13:5-6. State: We never suffer alone, because God is with us.
3. State that James also wrote to strengthen persecuted believers. Display the tear sheet you prepared and point to the first statement, *Recognize the source of your suffering.* Read James 1:13 and ask for responses to activity 6 on page 125. Ask, How should

a believer respond to temptation? (Fight and resist in God's power) State that James also identified suffering that God allowed to test believers. Ask, How should a believer respond to testing? (Submit and endure in order to learn what God wants to teach) Point to the next statement, *Be patient when you suffer.* Ask volunteers to read James 1:2-3; 5:7-8. Ask: What should our response be to suffering? What is the believer's assignment in suffering? What do we look forward to when we suffer? What is the fruit of patient endurance? Point to the next statement, *Practice an active faith.* Ask, How can we practice an active faith while being persecuted? (Look to God, not to circumstances.) Point to the next two statements, *Don't be judgmental* and *Don't complain.* Ask for responses to activity 10 on page 127. Point to the final statement, *Pray about your suffering.* Ask, Does prayer ensure that God will relieve our suffering? (No) Remind members that God does not always choose to heal sickness and relieve suffering during this lifetime, but He always meets our needs, gives us strength to endure, and shows compassion as we place our lives in His hands.

4. Call on the member enlisted to report on the material on 1 Peter. Then ask members to identify ways believers are persecuted for their faith in America and abroad. List these in two columns on a dry-erase board. Ask: Is persecution in America increasing? Why? Call on the member enlisted to report on the material on 2 Peter.

5. Read 1 John 2:15-16. Explain that John was not instructing believers to reject the physical world as evil but to renounce sin, selfishness, and evil desires. Read 1 John 4:4 and ask, Why is our victory ensured? Emphasize that the proper object of our faith is Jesus and that He is our hope during persecution. Read 1 John 4:18 and distinguish between believers' and unbelievers' views of God's coming judgment.

6. Divide members into five groups and give each group a marker and one of the tear sheets you prepared. Ask each group to review the corresponding subtopic under "Suffering in the Book of Revelation" (pp. 133–36) and to record ways the teaching would give hope to someone who is being persecuted for Christ. Call for reports.

7. State, We can draw several general conclusions from our study of evil and suffering. Display the placards as you summarize the ideas on pages 137–39.

8. Ask members to identify the three ways believers can respond to evil and suffering (pp. 139–42). When fighting evil is mentioned, call on the member enlisted to report on the suggestions.

Personalize

1. Ask for responses to activity 36 on page 142. Ask members to share ways they plan to respond to evil and suffering.

2. Direct members to "How Do You See It?" on page 155. Ask them to consider what they have learned during the study and to record their new responses in the session 6 column. Ask: Has your understanding of evil and suffering changed? What questions were answered for you?

3. Thank members for their participation. Close with prayer.

How Do You See It?

Indicate whether you agree (A) or disagree (D) with the following statements.

	Session 1	Session 6
1. Suffering is the result of not trusting God.		
2. Almost everyone experiences suffering, whether they are good or bad.		
3. Suffering is the result of sin.		
4. Suffering is sometimes the result of God's punishment for sin.		
5. God causes all natural disasters.		
6. God is in control of all things.		
7. God is removed from the human experience and doesn't relate to our suffering.		
8. Suffering is caused by the existence of evil.		
9. God temporarily permits evil in the world.		
10. Satan is the author of all evil.		
11. Evil and suffering are inseparably linked.		
12. Evil affects the guilty and the innocent.		
13. The Bible explains the reason for all suffering.		
14. God is intimately concerned when we suffer.		
15. God will bring about His plan even if we have to suffer.		

Lessons from the Pentateuch

Write personal implications of each lesson you learned from your study of evil and suffering in the Pentateuch.

Biblical Examples	Lessons Learned	Personal Implications
The Hebrews (Ex. 14:21); Pharaoh (Ex. 14:4); Moses (Ex. 4:11)	Yahweh is the only true God and the One ultimately responsible for the course of human history.	
Adam and Eve (Gen. 3:14-19); the Hebrews (Num. 21:4-6); Moses (Num. 20:12)	God is just in His actions, punishing the sinful and rewarding the faithful.	
The Hebrews (Ex. 3:7-8; Deut. 30:1-4)	God is loving and compassionate.	
Joseph (Gen. 45:7; 50:20)	God's basic intention for His people is always good.	
Foreigners, widows, and orphans (Deut. 24:17-18)	God expects His people to be concerned about suffering.	

What's Your Fear/Faith Factor?

Read each question and circle a number to indicate your response.

	Low Degree			High Degree	
1. To what degree do you worry about situations that are beyond your control?	1	2	3	4	5
2. To what degree are you spiritually prepared for the storms of life?	1	2	3	4	5
3. To what degree do you believe that Jesus ignores you when you face difficulties?	1	2	3	4	5
4. To what degree do you believe that Jesus is with you when you face trouble?	1	2	3	4	5
5. To what degree do you seek God's direction before making a decision?	1	2	3	4	5
6. To what degree do you trust God regardless of your circumstances?	1	2	3	4	5
7. To what degree does trouble cause you to doubt God?	1	2	3	4	5
8. To what degree do you experience panic?	1	2	3	4	5
9. To what degree do you experience peace?	1	2	3	4	5
10. To what degree do you believe that God is in control of all circumstances?	1	2	3	4	5

Total for questions 1, 3, 7, and 8: _____
Score of 4–8 = fervent faith/feeble fear. Score of 9–12 = faltering faith/flourishing fear.
Score of 13–20 = fear in full control.

Total for questions 2, 4, 5, 6, 9, and 10: _____
Score of 25–30 = rock-solid faith. Score of 15–24 = tentative trusting/fledgling fears.
Score of 6–14 = sinking-sand faith/full-gear fear.

Profiles of Persecution

Read your assigned profile and discuss with your small group: (1) What distinguishes this situation as suffering for the cause of Christ? (2) How did this event advance the gospel? (3) How does this profile challenge you to live and sacrifice for Christ?

Group 1: Jesus Is Lord

In December 2002 a gunman murdered three International Mission Board workers stationed at Jibla Baptist Hospital in Yemen. Hospital administrator Bill Koehn, surgeon Mart Myers, and purchasing manager Kathy Gariety were killed instantly.

The next day when Koehn and Myers were buried on the hospital grounds, several hundred Yemenis gathered to pay their respects. Mourners sang "He Is Lord" in Arabic and recited the Lord's Prayer.

God's Spirit is working to glorify God through His servants' lives and deaths. Through the efforts of these workers and their surviving colleagues, the Yemeni people have come to understand God's unconditional love for them. One Yemini man expressed the change he experienced: "Something is happening in my heart."

Lee Hixon, a remaining hospital worker, understands firsthand that when Jesus is Lord, the call to take the gospel to a needy people is preeminent: "The call of Jesus Christ to take the gospel personally to hurting individuals far outweighs the risks of living in a country like Yemen. If you had asked any of these people, 'Would you give your life to birth the church?' they would have replied, 'Absolutely.' "

International Mission Board, Southern Baptist Convention, *www.imb.org.*

Group 2: Purpose in Persecution

Most of the crowd never saw his face, but his story was unforgettable. Abdul*, a South Asian Muslim who had converted to Christianity, spoke at the 2004 Southern Baptist Convention. Abdul riveted the crowd's attention with his story of believers' persecution and martyrdom in his homeland. His witness and ministry there had sparked a spiritual awakening that had yielded more than 400,000 followers and 9,000 churches. But the advance of the kingdom had been costly. Abdul, who spoke with his back to the crowd, shared that nine evangelists had been murdered for their faith.

After Abdul returned home, the number of South Asians accepting Christ grew, but so did persecution. Soon 63 Christian men involved in Abdul's ministry were arrested and imprisoned. Instead of raising money to pay lawyers and court costs to free the men, believers gave money to the families of the men in prison. The men believed God had placed them in jail for a purpose.

Workers asked people to pray that the men would be able to endure their beatings and harsh conditions and that the prison guards and other prisoners would be open to the gospel through their witness.

*Name changed for security reasons. Adapted from an article by Shawn Hendricks, Baptist Press, © 2005 International Mission Board, Southern Baptist Convention, *www.imb.org.*